Bonds Between Atoms

ALAN HOLDEN

Bonds Between Atoms

1971
OXFORD UNIVERSITY PRESS
New York and Oxford

General Preface

This monograph is one of a connected series of three by the same author: *Stationary states*, *The nature of atoms*, and *Bonds between atoms*. Like its fellows, it was written for the Conference on New Instructional Materials in Physics, sponsored by the Commission on College Physics with the support of the National Science Foundation, and held at the University of Washington in the summer of 1965.

The purpose of the conference was to create effective ways of presenting physics to college students who are not preparing to become professional physicists. Such an audience might include prospective secondary-school physics teachers, prospective practitioners of other sciences, and those who wish to learn physics as one component of a liberal education.

The form of these, and of other monographs originating at that conference, implements a principle of experimental pedagogy promulgated there. Each monograph is 'multi-level': each consists of several sections arranged in order of increasing sophistication. Their authors hope that such papers can be fragmented for use in existing formal courses, or can be associated with other papers to provide the basis for new kinds of courses.

Contents

Foreword

THE field of inquiry into how atoms are bonded together to form molecules and solids crosses the borderlines between physics and chemistry, encompassing methods characteristic of both sciences. At one extreme, the inquiry is pursued with care and rigour into the simplest cases; at the other extreme, suggestions derived from the more careful inquiry are pushed with daring to provide qualitative insights into the complexities of chemical behaviour.

This monograph offers an introduction to both points of view and to the relationship between them. Dealing primarily with the physical nature of the simplest chemical bonds, it nevertheless examines a few molecules that are much more complicated, in order to point out the wide qualitative relevance of the more rigorous approach.

In developing its subject the monograph makes extensive use of simplified models. Indeed, taken as a whole, it constitutes an exercise in model making. In conducting such an activity, a difficult balance must be achieved between a sense of adventure on the one hand and a sense of responsibility on the other. The adventure is found in inventing the models and employing them in wide contexts. The responsibility resides in pursuing their implications relentlessly, to the point of calculating numerical values with their aid and comparing those values with the results of experimental measurements.

ALAN HOLDEN

Bonds Between Atoms

1. The Nature of Interatomic Bonds

'THE Parts of all homogeneal hard Bodies which fully touch one another, stick together very strongly. And for explaining how this may be, some have invented hooked Atoms, which is begging the Question ... I had rather infer from their Cohesion, that their Particles attract one another by some Force, which in immediate Contact is exceeding strong, at small distances performs the chymical Operations above-mentioned and reaches not far from the Particles with any sensible Effect ... There are therefore Agents in Nature able to make the Particles of Bodies stick together by very strong Attractions. And it is the Business of experimental Philosophy to find them out'. So wrote Sir Isaac Newton 260 years ago.

The pursuit of Sir Isaac's 'Business' over a quarter millenium has progressively found them out, wholly verifying the remarkable insight of this remarkable man. In 1945 Erwin Schrödinger, the principal architect of the means for completing the verification, could write that 'the atoms forming a molecule, whether there be few or many of them, are united by forces of exactly the same nature as the numerous atoms which build up a true solid, a crystal'. We know today that those forces are primarily electrostatic, the forces of attraction between electrical charges of opposite sign. The gravitational and magnetic forces that also operate in these unions are entirely negligible in comparison with the electrostatic.

In view of how little was known about atoms in Newton's time, his insight seems the more remarkable. Speculative minds had promulgated atomic theories of one sort and another for two thousand years. But Robert Boyle, Newton's contemporary, had been the first to urge the view that the world is made of *compounds* that can be decomposed into *elements*. The 'elements' of earlier times were not separate kinds of ultimate, undecomposable matter; they were aspects of a single neutral substance of which the world was made. These different aspects were produced by the combined application of definite and distinguishable formative principles on the neutral substance.

These ideas about the world arose from a doctrine of Aristotle that emphasized the distinction between 'substance' and 'form'.† The doctrine recognized four formative principles: hotness and dryness, and their opposites, coldness and wetness. By impressing those qualities in pairs on the single substance, the four primal forms of matter are produced according

† It has been suggested that Aristotle may have arrived at his doctrine by reflecting upon the activities of craftsmen and artists, who transmute formless matter into the objects that are of interest and use to man. Notice in any case that the Latin word *materia* meant wood-for-building.

to the following scheme:

$$dryness + hotness \rightarrow fire$$
$$dryness + coldness \rightarrow earth$$
$$wetness + hotness \rightarrow air$$
$$wetness + coldness \rightarrow water.$$

The many subsidiary differences between the forms in which these 'four elements' appear are reflections of the differences in the proportions and intensities with which the formative principles are applied.

Of all the ancient speculations about the construction of the world, this doctrine of the 'four elements' gave an especially powerful impulse and direction to early chemistry. The Arabs absorbed the doctrine when they conquered Egypt in the seventh century, using it to interpret the experiments stimulated by their active spirit of enquiry. The alchemy that developed at their hands rested on their belief that they could change any kind of matter into any other if they could but discover what formative principle, applied in what manner to the first kind, would produce the second.

The winning and modification of metals was an especially important preoccupation of the early investigators. Outstanding among them was Jabir ibn Hayyan (the 'Geber' of certain Latin texts) who added two more elements, mercury and sulphur, to the primal four. 'Mercury' was the principle giving metals their unalterable property, and 'sulphur' was the earthly impurity from which they could be cleansed. With increasing attention to the preparation of substances for medical use, a third element was added to the new list: 'salt', the residue that remained fixed after calcination. Indeed these three formed the *tria prima* of Paracelsus, the violent† man whose example inspired the reckless pharmacological experimentation of the sixteenth century.

As has happened so often in the history of science, and as happens today, without doubt, a body of theory later overthrown stimulates and organizes much valid observation of nature. When Boyle undertook his experiments in the middle of the seventeenth century, he could profit from the recorded results of many centuries of chemical work. Contemplating them, he wrote *The Sceptical Chymist*, published in 1661, which raised serious objections to the *tria prima*:

'There are some bodies from which it has not yet been made to appear that any degree of fire can separate either salt, or sulphur, or mercury, much less all three. Gold may be heated for months in a furnace without losing weight or altering, and yet one of its supposed constituents is volatile and another combustible. Neither can solvents separate any of the three principles from gold; the metal may be *added to*, and so brought into solution ... but the gold particles are present all the time; and the metal may be reduced to the same weight, of yellow, ponderous malleable substance it was before'.

† On receiving the professorship of medicine at Basle, Paracelsus' first public act was to burn the great handbooks of medicine by Galen and Avicenna.

After calling the *tria prima* in question in this fashion, Boyle proposed an alternative picture of chemical occurrences. He remarked upon the fact that many metals, lead and copper, for example, may be dissolved in acids and their properties entirely disguised in the resulting compound. Meeting with corpuscles of another kind, the corpuscles of metal may be more disposed to unite with them, he suggested, than to join with the particles forming the original metallic cluster. Thus from the coalition of two different corpuscles a new body may be formed 'as really one as either of the corpuscles before they were confounded'.

It was bold to suggest that mercury, a silvery metallic liquid, and sulphur, a readily fusible yellow solid, should combine to form the red mineral cinnabar, rather than the yellowish metal, gold. Indeed it seems equally bold today to advance the idea that the entire richness and diversity of the material world is formed by union of only a hundred kinds of atomic particles. Our notion that water is made from the particles of two gases, hydrogen and oxygen, in two-to-one proportion may seem no less preposterous than Aristotle's notion that water represents the impress of wetness and coldness on a matter-stuff, or than the notion of Thales of Miletus that water is itself the sole elementary source of the world.† But we have vastly more evidence to support today's fantastic contention than did the ancients. That evidence is the major content of the chemical knowledge acquired over the past three centuries.

But Boyle had left unanswered—in fact unstated—the question, 'Why and when do the particles join?' It was appropriate that Newton, who had made especially vivid use of the idea of *force* in the mechanics of visible objects, and who had fathered the law of universal gravitation, should appeal to the idea of force again to explain the cohesion of invisible particles in solids and also the interchanges of their allegiance in chemical reactions. But some good quantitative feeling, or perhaps some rough calculation that he does not describe, warned him that gravitational forces between the particles could not provide the explanation that he sought.

The electrostatic explanation that we accept today had to await the experiments with electricity that form a conspicuous scientific ornament of the nineteenth century. The previous century had witnessed a few notable discoveries, in particular that of the two kinds of electricity, positive and negative, by Charles Dufay in 1734. Dufay's observation that bodies with like electrification repel each other while those with unlike electrification attract each other had been made quantitative by Charles-Augustin Coulomb's brilliant use of his torsion balance near the end of the eighteenth century. But it was Alessandro Volta's announcement in 1800 of his electric

† In a famous experiment the seventeenth century Belgian physician and chemist, Jean Baptiste van Helmont, believed that he had verified Thales' doctrine by growing a willow shoot in dried earth and watering it regularly until it had gained many pounds in weight without receiving any other nutrient that van Helmont could discern. Ironically, this was the man who also discovered carbon dioxide, in other experiments.

battery, 'which in a word provides an unlimited charge or imposes a perpetual action or impulsion on the electric fluid', that made possible the crucial chemical experiments.

In that same year William Nicholson noticed the products of electrolysis of river water appearing at the free ends of wires connected to a voltaic pile. Hence one of the first acts of Sir Humphry Davy, on becoming director of the laboratory at the Royal Institution in London the following year, was to construct a large battery of the sort Volta had described. With it he followed up Nicholson's observation vigorously over the next five years, with results that he symmarized in the following words.

'Hydrogen, the alkaline substances, the metals, and certain metallic oxides are attracted by negatively electrified metallic surfaces and repelled by positively electrified metallic surfaces; and contrariwise, oxygen and acid substances are attracted by positively electrified metallic surfaces and repelled by negatively electrified surfaces; and these attractive and repulsive forces are sufficiently energetic to destroy or suspend the usual operation of elective affinity'.

It was then natural to assume further that 'the usual operation of elective affinity' is itself electrostatic, the attraction of oppositely charged atoms of different species. Davy in England, and Jöns Berzelius in Sweden, both soon came to this view, and the latter formulated an electrochemical theory of the formation of compounds, published in 1814, which put forward this 'dualistic hypothesis' in explanation of all chemical action. Berzelius even extended these ideas into organic chemistry, proposing that groups of atoms can form compound 'radicals', positive and negative, which then join together as elements would.

But it is clear that, however well such a theory may fit the observations on substances that can be brought into solution and electrolysed, it cannot explain all the interatomic forces found in nature. From measurements on gaseous hydrogen and oxygen and their reaction to form water vapour it was becoming increasingly clear in Berzelius' own time that these gases are both composed of molecules of which each contains two atoms tightly joined. Berzelius long opposed this conclusion because he could not find in his dualistic theory any binding force between two identical atoms. But the idea of diatomic molecules was unavoidable, and binding force there must be.

The origin of the forces between identical atoms has been found only in this century, with the identification of the electron by J. J. Thomson in 1897 and the development of pictures of the inner structure of atoms made possible by that discovery. It turns out that such seemingly diverse interatomic attractions as those found in hydrogen molecules, in metals, and in crystalline argon can all be convincingly explained in electrostatic terms. The next chapter will provide a qualitative discussion of the various ways in which the electronic constitution of atoms can operate to provide bonds between them, and the rest of this monograph will pursue the same questions more quantitatively and in greater detail.

2. The Classification of Bonding

IN talking about interatomic bonds, and about the aggregations of atoms assembled by them, it is helpful to make classifications—suggestive, not hard and fast—of as many sorts as come to mind. The bonds might be divided, for example, into two classes; those between similar atoms, such as the bond between two hydrogen atoms that ties them together in a hydrogen molecule, and those between dissimilar atoms, such as the bond between sodium and chlorine in sodium chloride. And the world's solids might be divided into two classes: those that melt into electrically conducting liquids, and those that melt into electrically insulating liquids. The proposed classification of interatomic bonds is clearly exhaustive; the classification of solids is not, for many solids decompose into new materials at temperatures below their melting point. But these classifications are simple, and useful for a start.

If two atoms come close to each other, they will not remain unaffected by each other. If they belong to different atomic species, one may accommodate electronic charges somewhat more readily than the other. Charge may flow from the one to the other, leaving the one with a net positive charge and giving the other a net negative charge. Then the two partly *ionized* atoms will attract each other electrostatically, providing the bond visualized by Davy and Berzelius as the last chapter described. In the extreme case each atom of one species completely transfers one electron to an atom of the other species, and the ions can be expected to assemble about one another in such a way that each ion is as near as it can be to as many ions of the other species as possible, and as far as possible from the similarly charged ions of its own species.

In a solid so formed, an ion has no preference for a particular one of the ions of the other species. Molecules, formed by pairs of ions, cannot be unambiguously identified in the solid. In crystalline sodium chloride, for example, the ions are arranged as shown in Fig. 2.1: each ion is immediately surrounded by six ions of the other species.

As the figure shows, the ions in such a solid are packed together too tightly to move past one another; they can only vibrate about their average positions. But when the solid is melted, the ions will be able to drift through the liquid as they could not through the solid. If an electric field is applied to the liquid, the ions of the two species will drift in opposite directions. When they reach the electrodes that establish the field, the negative ions will discharge their extra electrons to the positively charged electrode, and the positive ions will acquire from the negative electrode the electrons that they lost when they became ions.

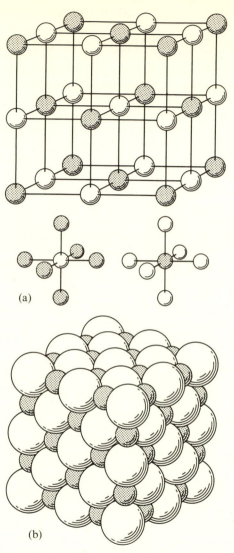

FIG. 2.1. In solid sodium chloride, each negative ion is immediately surrounded by six positive ions, and each positive ion by six negative ions, as shown at (a). Diagrams of atomic arrangements in crystals usually show just the locations of the centres of the atoms, so that the arrangements can be seen more readily. The diagram (b) shows more truly how the ions pack together. It was drawn by William Barlow, who suggested more than seventy years ago that the atoms in sodium chloride might take this arrangement in the solid. Objections were raised then that the structure does not portray the atoms as associated in diatomic molecules. But studies of sodium chloride crystals by X-ray diffraction have since shown that Barlow was right. In the solid the molecules, not the structure, had to be discarded. His diagram also shows correctly that one species of ions is larger than the other.

In this way neutral atoms of the two species will accumulate at the opposite electrodes; and if they cannot combine with the material of the electrode, they will combine with one another in whatever way is characteristic of them. Molten sodium chloride, for example, can be electrolysed to yield sodium metal and chlorine gas. Since the drifting of the ions carries a drift of charge, a current flows; and the amounts of metal and gas produced are proportional to the product of the current and the time during which it has flowed. Thus, in principle at least, the fact that a solid is ionically bonded can be ascertained by observing that it is an electrical insulator that melts to an electrically conducting liquid whose conduction is accompanied by electrolysis.

If, on the other hand, two similar atoms come close to each other, there is no reason to expect charge to flow permanently from one to the other, for the two atoms are indistinguishable in kind, and there is no evidence that it does. Nevertheless they do attract each other, and often that fact can be explained by supposing that electronic charges move back and forth between the two atoms. Then instantaneously each has a charge opposite to that of the other. Moreover, while the electrons are moving they are instantaneously between the two atoms, and there they provide a cloud of negative charge that attracts both the atoms because, having contributed the negative charges in the cloud, the atoms bear net positive charges.

When two similar atoms join in this way, the attraction between them is called a *covalent* bond. Their electronic charges bond them in both these ways, as Chapters 5, 6, and 7 analyse in more detail. The electrons try to decrease their total energy: the sum of their kinetic energy and their potential energy. Their potential energy is lower when they are close to one or the other of the positively charged nuclei. But their kinetic energy is lower if they can range over a wider space, because then their de Broglie wavelength λ is longer, and their momentum $p = h/\lambda$ is smaller.[†]

Hence there is a competition between the decrease of kinetic energy and the increase of potential energy of the electrons when they make wider excursions from the atoms. When two atoms permit an electron to visit them, and so to decrease the electronic kinetic energy, the electron may find that its total energy is lowered by visiting back and forth. In order to make such visiting worthwhile, each atom must offer to the electron a permitted state whose energy is low enough, and which is not already occupied by another electron. The latter qualification, coming from the *exclusion principle*, is the more stringent: more than any other single principle, it distinguishes the bonds that are possible from those that are not.[†]

Thus in a covalent bond two similar atoms are held together by electrons that exchange places between them. Part of the time that exchange gives the atoms opposite net charges, and the rest of the time it leaves both of them with a net positive charge that is attracted toward a concentration of negative

[†] The connections between kinetic energy and the de Broglie wavelength, and the exclusion principle, are described in *Stationary states*, Chapters 6 and 9.

charge between them, as Fig. 2.2 suggests. This is usually a localized phenomenon. The electrons participating in the bond are contributed by both of the bonded atoms, and commonly they extend their allegiance no further; the bond is localized between the two atoms. Each atom may be bonded to other atoms also, by other electrons. But each of these bonds can usually be pictured quite separately, engaging different electrons that do not move from one bond into another. In many cases the covalent bonding that

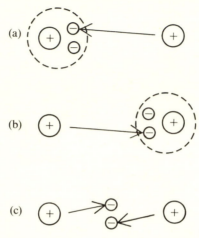

FIG. 2.2. Three formal arrangements of two electrons in a hydrogen molecule. When both electrons are near one or the other nucleus (a and b), there is a net negative charge within the dotted line, and the two atoms attract each other as two ions would. When the electrons are between the nuclei (c), they attract both nuclei toward them, and thus toward each other.

links atom to atom comes to an end with relatively few atoms, to form a molecule; and then the bonding of molecule to molecule, to form a liquid or a solid, originates in forces whose character is not covalent. In diatomic molecules such as those composing hydrogen gas, there is only one covalent bond per molecule. In a molecule of the hydrocarbons of which paraffin consists, from twenty to fifty carbon atoms are covalently linked in chains, and hydrogen atoms are covalently bonded to them. The modern plastic, polythene, consists of similar molecules, but each contains many hundred atoms linked together. Finally, in a crystal of diamond, the constituent carbon atoms are all joined by covalent bonds, as Fig. 2.3 shows, into a single gigantic molecule.

Notice, however, that since the electrons participating in the covalent bonding of a molecule remain within the confines of the molecule, they cannot drift through the solid, and the solid is an electrical insulator. Moreover, when the solid is heated it will usually melt into electrically neutral molecules, not charged ions, and hence the liquid will also be an insulator. Yellow crystalline sulphur, for instance, melts to a light-yellow insulating liquid, each of whose molecules contains eight sulphur atoms.

There are exceptions to this covalent behaviour, easily understood. When two atoms of different species are bonded, the bond may be changed from the purely covalent toward the ionic. If the energy of the state offered by one

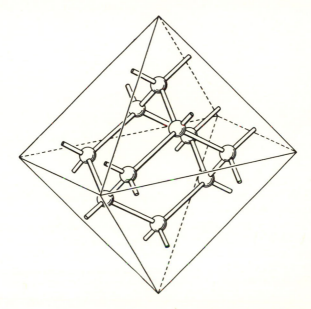

FIG. 2.3. In diamond, each carbon atom is immediately surrounded by four others, held to it by strong covalent bonds directed toward the four corners of a regular tetrahedron. The resulting network of bonds makes a diamond crystal a single giant molecule, and the bonds' strength gives to diamond its extreme hardness.

atom is slightly lower than that of the state offered by the other, the average electronic charge will be displaced toward the atom offering the state of lower energy. When the material is melted, the thermal agitation may dissociate some of the molecules into ions, and the melt may therefore show ionic conduction of electricity.

The displacement of charge toward one of the two bonded atoms gives to the pair of atoms a *dipole moment*, as Fig. 2.4 points out. Such dipole moments within molecules are important contributors to the bonds between the molecules in a liquid or solid. The force between two dipoles varies not only with their separation but also with their relative orientation, as Fig. 2.5 shows. Since favourable relative orientations will afford lower electrostatic energies than unfavourable orientations, the molecules will tend to

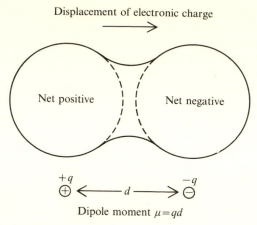

Displacement of electronic charge

Net positive   Net negative

$+q$ $-q$
$\oplus \longleftarrow d \longrightarrow \ominus$

Dipole moment $\mu = qd$

FIG. 2.4. If electronic charge is displaced toward one of two bonded atoms, the pair acquires a dipole moment.

assemble into a favourable arrangement, held together by *dipole–dipole* forces. If the molecules are large and contain several species of atoms, the stray fields from the individual dipole moments of the several bonds can add together to give a force whose spatial dependence is quite complicated. Moreover, when there are many such dipoles, the total force holding one molecule to another can be rather large. Partly for this reason, large and complicated organic molecules often form crystals that melt at moderately high temperatures.

Even when the bonds have no dipole moment, however, the molecules attract one another. The picture of the covalent bond formalized in Fig. 2.2 offers two reasons for this attraction. In the first place, the concentration

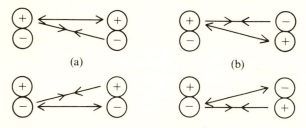

(a)   (b)

FIG. 2.5. Two arrangements of two dipoles. In arrangement (a), the positive charge in the dipole at left is slightly nearer to the positive charge than to the negative charge in the dipole at right, and hence that charge repels the dipole slightly. Similarly, the negative charge in the dipole at left also repels the dipole at right, and thus the two dipoles repel each other. In arrangement (b), the attractions between the charges slightly outweigh the repulsions, and the two dipoles attract each other.

of negative charge midway between two equal positive charges gives the bond a 'quadrupole moment' (Fig. 2.6). Again, favourable orientations permit an attraction between two quadrupoles, but that attraction is weaker and falls off more rapidly with distance than the attraction between two dipoles.

In the second place, the flow of charge back and forth between the two atoms, so that each is alternately positive and negative, gives the bond an oscillating dipole moment. If such oscillations are properly phased in

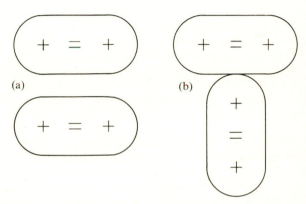

Fig. 2.6. Two arrangements of the quadrupoles in two covalently bonded molecules: (a) higher energy (less favourable), and (b) lower energy (more favourable).

neighbouring molecules, the fluctuating dipole moments will make the molecules attract one another, much as do the fixed dipole moments in some of the arrangements of Fig. 2.5.

It turns out that this second sort of contribution will always be present, not only between molecules but also between atoms. The analysis carried out in Chapter 4 shows that the force increases with the *polarizability* of the molecules or atoms—the ratio of the dipole moment induced by an electric field to the magnitude of the inducing field. Since the polarizability of an atom or molecule increases in rough proportion to its volume, as the next chapter shows, these forces tend to be larger between larger molecules.

The temperature at which a material boils provides a rough qualitative measure of the forces between its molecules: in order to boil the material, enough energy must be supplied to it to separate its molecules. Table 2.1 shows how the properties of some organic substances support the preceding picture of how their molecules interact. The hydrocarbons, which have no dipole moment, boil at much lower temperatures than the corresponding alcohols, which are polar. Furthermore, in both series of compounds, the boiling points increase as the size of the molecules increases.

TABLE 2.1   *Boiling points in kelvins*

Hydrocarbons		Alcohols	
Methane (CH$_4$)	112	Methyl (CH$_3$OH)	340
Ethane (C$_2$H$_6$)	200	Ethyl (C$_2$H$_5$OH)	351
Propane (C$_3$H$_8$)	228	Propyl (C$_3$H$_7$OH)	370
Butane (C$_4$H$_{10}$)	274	Butyl (C$_4$H$_9$OH)	390

There are still other electrostatic effects that will contribute to the bonding between molecules. If fixed ionic charges are present, they will tend to polarize neighbouring atoms and molecules, to shift the centres of charge in them slightly so that they acquire dipole moments even if they had none in the absence of the ions, as Fig. 2.7 suggests. These dipole moments then exert forces on one another and on the ions responsible for them. Similarly, though less strongly, fixed dipole moments in some bonds will induce dipole moments elsewhere.

Collectively these electrostatic forces from so-called stray fields are usually termed *van der Waals forces*,† and are distinguished from strictly ionic

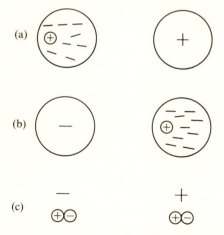

FIG. 2.7. Two oppositely charged ions induce dipoles in each other. The positive ion attracts the negatively charged cloud in the negative ion (a), and the negative ion repels the negatively charged cloud in the positive ion (b). The resulting dipoles in the two ions are so arranged that they contribute an additional attractive force to the force between the ionic charges.

† The Dutch physical chemist, Johannes van der Waals, was the first to take into account explicitly the effect of these attractive forces on the properties of gases.

forces, as well as from covalent bonding forces. The particular sort of van der Waals force that is due to the correlation in the phases of oscillating dipoles is often distinguished as the *dispersion force*. The distinction is useful because the dispersion force stands somewhat apart from other van der Waals forces in three respects. In the first place it is the only attractive force that operates between isolated neutral atoms—atoms that are not ionized or covalently bonded. In the second place it is independent of the relative orientations of the participants (except insofar as their polarizabilities depend on direction) and it is *additive*. Each atom or molecule can be thought to contain a host of oscillating dipoles, each properly phased to interact attractively with an oscillating dipole in each companion atom or molecule. In the third place the force is always present, even between ions and between the inner electronic cores of atoms that are covalently bonded by their outer electrons.

But all the van der Waals forces are significantly weaker than ionic and covalent bonding forces. Moreover they fall off more rapidly with distance. The force between two ions separated by a distance r falls off as $1/r^2$. Between two permanent dipoles, with fixed relative orientations, the force falls off as $1/r^4$; and between two atoms interacting with the dispersion force, it falls off as $1/r^7$. Their smaller magnitude and more rapid disappearance with distance permit a solid bonded by these forces to melt at a lower temperature than ionically and covalently bonded materials. The melting point of solid argon, whose crystals are made of closepacked neutral atoms, is 83 K, whereas potassium chloride, the ionic crystal formed from the two elements with atomic numbers one greater and one less than argon, melts at 1049 K.

Return now to the picture of covalent bonding, and in particular to the argument that an electron will reduce its kinetic energy by extending its excursions as far as it can. Evidently that argument will account for the fact that the electrons in metals roam throughout the material. The roaming electrons provide a sea of negative charge in which swim the positive ions that have contributed those electrons. The negatively charged sea between the ions holds them together, and the attraction of the ions in turn prevents the sea from flowing away.

Then why are not all materials metallic? Looking at the periodic table, you will find that most of the elements do solidify as metals, and the solid metals melt into metallic liquids. In nonmetallic materials the roaming of the electrons would increase their potential energy more than it would decrease their kinetic energy; it would require them to spend too much time too far from the positively charged nuclei.

Whenever the electrons can make those excursions, roaming from atom to atom indiscriminately to give the liquid or solid metallic properties, an electric field will make the electrons drift. The resulting 'electronic' conduction is distinguishable from ionic conduction by the fact that the nuclei do not drift, and thus no products of electrolysis are deposited at the electrodes.

In such a case, even in the liquid, the electrons can drift so much more readily than the nuclei and their surrounding cores of bound electrons that the conductivity is still electronic.

There are some materials whose molecules give some of their electrons freedom to roam within the confines of a molecule, but not to roam from molecule to molecule. In a molecule of benzene, for example, six electrons are free to roam about a ring of six carbon atoms. But the electrons cannot escape from the molecule, and hence benzene is an electrical insulator.

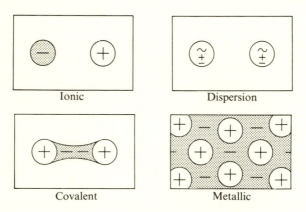

Fig. 2.8. Memory aids for the four extreme types of bonding.

In summary, it is conventional to distinguish four extreme types of bonds: (1) ionic bonds, forming 'ionic' solids; (2) covalent bonds within molecules, or within complex ions such as SO_4, and sometimes linking together the atoms in an entire crystal to form solids such as diamond; (3) van der Waals forces, forming 'molecular' solids from neutral atoms and molecules; and (4) the 'metallic' bonds characteristic of metals. With the understanding that its pictures must be interpreted in terms of the preceding discussion, Fig. 2.8 offers aids for remembering the distinctions between these four extreme types of bonds. But any such classification is necessarily rough. Thus a covalent bond between two different species of atoms always has some ionic character. By polarizing its partner, an ion will usually give to an ionic bond a partly covalent character. The accumulation of charge density along lines between adjacent atoms in a metal will often give the metallic bond a partly localized property. The weak dispersion force, hard to discern in the presence of stronger forces, is always present. And the origin of all these forces is ultimately the same: the electrostatic attraction between positively charged atomic nuclei and negatively charged electrons.

Matter in the solid state exhibits especially clearly the distinctions of the four classes of bonds outlined in this chapter. The form of order adopted by

TABLE 2.2 *Properties of the solid*

Solid Type	Crystal Units	Binding Force	Optical	Electrical	Thermal	Mechanical	Examples
Ionic	Simple and complex ions	Electrostatic attraction of oppositely charged ions	Transparent, or coloured by characteristic absorption of ions	Insulators, forming conducting solutions in ionizing solvents	Fairly high melting, to form ions	Hardness increases with ionic charge; break by cleavage	Sodium chloride, calcite, ammonium sulphate
Adamantine	Group IV elements; III–V and II–VI compounds	Covalent, sometimes partly ionic	Transparent, high refractive index; or opaque	Semiconductors except diamond; insoluble	Very high melting	Very hard; break by cleavage	Diamond, carborundum, zinc blende
Molecular	Rare gas atoms; molecules	Dispersion and multipole forces	Transparent, and like its molten form	Insulators; dissolve in nonionizing solvents	Fairly low melting	Soft and plastically deformable	Argon, paraffins, calomel
Metallic	Positive ions and 'free' electrons	Attraction between ions and electron 'gas'	Opaque and reflecting	Electronic conductors; soluble in acids to form salts	Moderately high melting; good heat conductors	Tough and ductile, except tungsten	Copper, iron, sodium

the atoms when they assemble into crystals is often diagnostic of many details in the character of the interatomic bonding. Some of the more conspicuous properties of solids are suggested in Table 2.2, which lists the four classes.

The listed properties, however, can at best be only illustrative. There are many exceptions to the extreme behaviour outlined in the table. Some properties vary greatly with small amounts of impurities in the solid, and the study of their influence has become an important branch of 'solid-state physics'.

PROBLEMS

2.1   Why do many molecular crystals have low densities?

2.2   When a solid contains several sorts of bonds:
(a) Would you expect its melting point to be determined ordinarily by its weakest bonds or its strongest bonds?
(b) Under what circumstances would you expect to find exceptions to your answers to (a)?

3. Ionic Bonds

THE dualistic theory of chemical combination proposed by Davy and Berzelius, although it is not as simply and widely applicable as they had hoped, explains quite successfully in a qualitative way the formation of chemical compounds by atomic species from opposite sides of the periodic table. At the turn of the century, even before Ernest Rutherford developed the picture of the planetary atom, J. J. Thomson had suggested that the electrons are arranged in groups or layers in an atom, and that the number of electrons in the outermost layer largely determines the chemical properties of the species.

According to Thomson, the atoms of the rare gases must contain especially stable arrangements of electrons. An atom with one electron less than a rare-gas atom, for example chlorine, tends to acquire an extra electron and so to form a negative ion. An atom with one more electron, for example sodium, readily loses it, to form a positive ion. Atoms that readily lose electrons will combine chemically with atoms that tend to acquire electrons, a picture now familiar to all who have studied elementary chemistry.

It is interesting to examine some aspects of this theory in a more quantitative way. Consider, for example, the alkali halides—the compounds formed by the alkali metals Li, Na, K, Rb, and Cs, with the halogens F, Cl, Br, and I. The elementary picture portrays spherical ions having opposite charges of $+e$ and $-e$ (where e is the magnitude of the electronic charge, $1 \cdot 6 \times 10^{-19}$ coulombs) attracting each other electrostatically. It can be examined quite successfully without recourse to quantum mechanics, and by using a simple electrostatic argument it can be made to yield close quantitative agreement with experiment. But it needs some modification nevertheless, as this chapter will show.

In experimental fact, when a solid alkali halide is vaporized, the oppositely charged ions pair off into diatomic molecules, and the data obtained from the vapour can be used to verify the picture. For several such molecules, Table 3.1 shows the experimentally determined distances r_0 (in ångströms) between the centres of the ions, and the experimentally determined energy D (in electron volts) required to separate the ions by an infinite distance.† Electrostatic theory says that each spherically symmetric distribution of charge should behave toward charges outside it as if its total charge were concentrated at its centre. Hence the picture predicts that $D = e^2/4\pi\epsilon_0 r_0$, and the last column of the table verifies the prediction.

† The units employed are described in the associated Discussion 3.1, Units. 'Infinite distance' means here so far that they interact negligibly.

TABLE 3.1   *Molecules of alkali halides*

	r_0 (Angstroms)	D (Electron Volts)	$4\pi\epsilon_0 D r_0/e^2$
KF	2·55	5·8	1·03
KCl	2·79	4·92	0·95
KBr	2·94	4·64	0·95
KI	3·23	4·51	1·01
NaCl	2·51	5·54	0·96
NaBr	2·64	5·33	0·98
NaI	2·90	5·14	1·09

Discussion 3.1

UNITS

By employing S.I. units our formulas will yield energies in joules, and electric fields in newtons per coulomb. For greater convenience in different physical and chemical contexts, different units of distance and of energy are often used, and it is helpful to become acquainted with some of them. The *ångström unit of length* is widely used in quoting distances of atomic size.

$$1 \text{ angstrom } (1 \text{ Å}) = 10^{-10} \text{ metre } (10^{-10} \text{ m}).$$

A unit of energy commonly used in speaking of the behaviour of matter on an atomic scale is the *electron volt*, the kinetic energy acquired by an electron accelerated through a potential difference of one volt.

$$1 \text{ electron volt } (1 \text{ eV}) = 1·6 \times 10^{-19} \text{ joules (J)}.$$

In speaking of bulk matter, on the other hand, chemists especially use as a unit of energy the kilogramme-calorie per mole—the heat-equivalent of the energy per molecule, reckoned for Avogadro's number $(6·03 \times 10^{23})$ of molecules.

$$1 \text{ kilogramme-calorie } (1 \text{ kcal}) = 4·18 \times 10^3 \text{ joules}.$$

It is convenient to bear in mind the approximate conversion factor

$$1 \text{ eV per particle } = 23 \text{ kcal per mole of particles}.$$

This conversion factor is calculated by the following steps:

$$1 \text{ eV/particle } = 6 \times 10^{23} \text{ eV/mol} = 6 \times 10^{23} \times 1·6 \times 10^{-19} \text{ J/mol}$$

$$= 9·6 \times 10^4 \text{ J/mol} = \frac{9·6 \times 10^4}{4·18 \times 10^3} \text{ kcal/mol} = 23 \text{ kcal/mol}.$$

Look now at the relationship between these measurements and some others that bear upon them. For example, measurements of the *ionization energy* of sodium show that 5·1 eV of energy is required to remove to an infinite distance one electron from an isolated atom of sodium. Measurements of the *electron affinity* of chlorine show that 3·7 eV of energy is returned when one electron is returned from an infinite distance to an isolated atom of chlorine. At first glance, passing one electron from a sodium atom to a chlorine atom may seem unfavourable, to the extent of 1·4 eV per molecule of sodium chloride.

You are rescued by noticing that, if the sodium chloride molecule were formed in this way, the two ions would still be separated by a great distance. For the purpose of quantitative argument the formation of the ionic bond

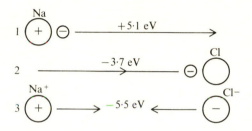

FIG. 3.1. The bond between sodium and chlorine is almost purely ionic because the dissociation energy (3) is so much greater than the difference between the ionization potential (1) of sodium and the electron affinity (2) of chlorine. The energies are given in electron volts.

in sodium chloride could be imagined to occur in the three stages shown in Fig. 3.1. In the approach of the two ions to their final separation (stage 3) there can be a gain of energy more than compensating the net loss in the first two stages. The energy in stage 3 is clearly the dissociation energy in Table 3.1.

Now examine some simple modifications that must be introduced into the preceding model of the ionic bond. For example, the calculation summarized in Table 3.1 assumes that the atoms are infinitely hard, incompressible balls, attracting each other until they bump. Of course their structure is not really as rigid as that: all matter, even solid matter, is compressible. Fig. 3.2 shows the difference between the picture lying behind the calculation and the picture suggested by the compressibility of atoms. The attraction between the oppositely charged ions pulls them together until the repulsive force between them balances the attractive force, and the energy of their interaction is a minimum.

The origins of this repulsive force usually lie largely in the properties of electrons that are summarized in the exclusion principle. As the two ions approach each other, the electrons in each are more and more required to occupy space already inhabited by the electrons in its partner. In order to do so, they must find states in that space. But the states permitted to a bound electron are discrete and definite, each with a definite energy; and only two electrons, with their spins opposed, can occupy any one of them. Thus the electrons in the approaching ions are forced into states whose energies increase rapidly as the distance between the ions decreases.

Look now for a way to take this repulsive interaction into quantitative account. Although no theory so simple as that of the electrostatic attraction is available to guide you in studying the repulsion, you can resort to a device that is often employed in similar situations. Choose a mathematical expression

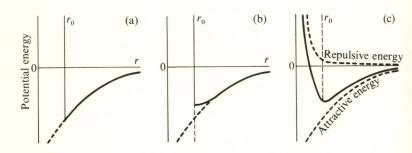

Fig. 3.2. The assumption that two oppositely charged ions are hard spheres, attracting each other until they bump, yields the energy diagram (a). But in fact the ions feel a repulsive force, which increases rapidly as they approach each other, so that the attraction is partly offset by a repulsion before the atoms bump (b). The truth is better represented (c) as the sum of a repulsive energy and an attractive energy, which reaches a minimum at the actual separation of the ions.

that has a general behaviour suitable for representing a repulsive force, and that affords enough adjustability to accommodate some variation from one molecule to another.

In this case it is suitable to add to the attractive potential energy, $-e^2/4\pi\epsilon_0 r$, a repulsive potential energy, B/r^n, where r, the distance between the ions, is allowed to vary. The undetermined coefficient B and exponent n confer the desired adjustability: the former measures the strength of the repulsion and the latter measures the sharpness with which the repulsive force increases as the ions approach each other. The energy of the pair of ions at any separation, relative to that of the infinitely separated ions, then becomes

$$E = -e^2/4\pi\epsilon_0 r + B/r^n. \tag{3.1}$$

In order to make comparisons of this expression with experiment, the two constants B and n must be determined by resort to two properties of the pair of ions, independently measured or calculated. One property available for this purpose is the experimental interatomic separation r_0 listed in Table 3.1.

Since E must reach a minimum when $r = r_0$, B can be put in terms of r_0 in the way shown in Discussion 3.2. Eqn (3.1) then yields an expected dissociation energy at the actual separation r_0

$$D = \frac{e^2}{4\pi\epsilon_0 r_0}\left(1 - \frac{1}{n}\right). \tag{3.2}$$

Discussion 3.2

EQUILIBRIUM SEPARATION OF IONS

The energy of interaction of two ions, at any separation r, is well represented by the expression

$$E = -e^2/4\pi\epsilon_0 r + B/r^n.$$

The equilibrium separation r_0 is attained when E reaches a minimum. This fact enables the constant B to be determined in terms of r_0 as follows. The derivative of E with respect to r is

$$\frac{dE}{dr} = \frac{e^2}{4\pi\epsilon_0 r^2} - \frac{nB}{r^{n+1}}.$$

Setting that derivative equal to zero at $r = r_0$ gives

$$\frac{nB}{r_0^{n+1}} = \frac{e^2}{4\pi\epsilon_0 r_0^2}, \quad \text{or} \quad B = \frac{e^2 r_0^{n-1}}{4\pi\epsilon_0 n}.$$

The energy E when $r = r_0$ is the dissociation energy of the molecule:

$$-D = \frac{-e^2}{4\pi\epsilon_0 r_0} + \frac{B}{r_0^n},$$

where D is the energy required to separate the two ions. Using the value of B just found,

$$-D = \frac{-e^2}{4\pi\epsilon_0 r_0}\left(1 - \frac{1}{n}\right).$$

In other words, at the equilibrium separation, the repulsive energy is equal to the nth part of the attractive energy.

Clearly the repulsive energy, by reducing the expected dissociation energy, will damage the agreement with experiment shown in Table 3.1, by an amount depending on the value of n. Suitable values of n have been found by examining the compressibilities of crystalline alkali halides; they lie between 8 and 10. Hence the calculated values of D will now be smaller than the experimental values by about ten per cent.

Fortunately there is a second important modification of our model of ionic bonding that will increase the calculated attractive energy, and so tend to compensate the repulsive energy. As the preceding chapter pointed out, each ion will polarize its partner, and the dipole moments so induced will be

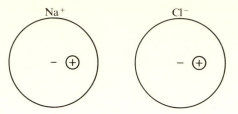

FIG. 3.3. The net charge on each ion polarizes the other ion, and the resulting dipoles are so oriented that they attract each other.

favourably oriented to provide an additional attractive force between them (Fig. 3.3).

In order to find the size of this effect, it is necessary to examine first the *polarizability* of atoms and ions. The polarizability α of an atom, an important quantity in many calculations, is the magnitude of the dipole moment μ that an electric field $\mathbf{E}$ will induce in an atom per unit electric field:

$$\boldsymbol{\mu} = \alpha\mathbf{E}. \tag{3.3}$$

The dipole moment of a pair of equal and opposite charges is defined in turn as the product of the separation of the charges by the magnitude of the charge on either, and the definition can be extended, as in Discussion 3.3, to apply to a collection of any number of charges.

Discussion 3.3

DIPOLE MOMENTS

The dipole moment of the charges $+q$ and $-q$, separated by a distance d, is defined as $\mu = qd$. Evidently in a fixed coordinate system whose x axis lies along the line determined by the locations x_1 and x_2 of the two charges, the preceding definition is equivalent to the expression $\mu = q(x_1 - x_2)$, or

$$\mu = q_1 x_1 + q_2 x_2$$

where

$$q_1 = -q_2 = q.$$

When there are many charges, of different magnitudes and signs, $q_1, q_2, \ldots$ whose positions are (x_1, y_1, z_1), (x_2, y_2, z_2), $\ldots$ and the total charge on the collection is zero, the total dipole moment can be defined in an analogous way as a vector whose components are

$$\mu_x = q_1 x_1 + q_2 x_2 + \ldots,$$

$$\mu_y = q_1 y_1 + q_2 y_2 + \ldots,$$

$$\mu_z = q_1 z_1 + q_2 z_2 + \ldots.$$

The picture to hold in mind while using eqn (3.3) in the present case is that suggested in Fig. 3.4. The atomic model consists of a nucleus with a charge $+Ze$ (where Z is the atomic number of the atom), which is embedded in a spherically symmetrical cloud of negative charge totalling $-Ze$ contributed by the electrons. When the atom is undisturbed, the nucleus is at the centre of the electronic cloud and the atom has no dipole moment. When an electric field $\mathbf{E}$ is applied to the atom, the cloud shifts so that the nucleus lies a distance a from its centre.

To answer the question of how large a dipole moment that shift produces is difficult if we try to take into account how the density of charge within the

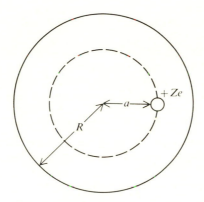

FIG. 3.4. To estimate the polarizability of an atom, approximate its structure by a uniform cloud of negative charge of radius R surrounding a positively charged nucleus lodged off-centre.

electron cloud varies as one proceeds through it. But to make a rough calculation, sufficient for this purpose and many others, a greatly simplified model of the electronic cloud will avail. Take the charge $-Ze$ as uniformly distributed within a sphere of radius R.

Then you can reason as follows. Your picture will be simpler, and your calculation the same, if you imagine the nucleus moving in a fixed cloud rather than a cloud moving with respect to a fixed nucleus. The force exerted on the nucleus by the field is $Ze\mathbf{E}$. That force will shift the nucleus until it is balanced by a restoring force, which can be taken as $k\mathbf{a}$, a force proportional to the displacement $\mathbf{a}$, where k is some force constant, soon to be estimated.†

---

† The validity of this assumption is limited to the small displacements produced by small forces. In such a case the functional relation between force and displacement can be expanded in a power series in the displacement, and the function can be approximated by retaining the first non-vanishing term of the series, which will here be the linear term. The maximum values of the displacement a turn out indeed to be small, of the order of one-tenth of an ionic radius.

But the dipole moment of the atom is now $\mu = Ze\mathbf{a} = \alpha\mathbf{E}$. When the displacement $\mathbf{a}$ is eliminated between this equation and the equation $Ze\mathbf{E} = k\mathbf{a}$, the polarizability is given in terms of the force constant by

$$\alpha = \frac{(Ze)^2}{k}. \tag{3.4}$$

In order to estimate the magnitude of the force constant, assume that the restoring force on the nucleus is simply the electrostatic force exerted on it by the charge cloud, which tries to move the nucleus back to the centre. It is a familiar result of electrostatic theory that a charge that is wholly inside

TABLE 3.2   *Polarizabilities of ions*

Ion	$(\alpha/4\pi\epsilon_0)^{\frac{1}{3}}$ (Angstroms)	Radius (Angstroms)
Na^+	0·91	0·97
K^+	1·10	1·33
Mg^{++}	0·87	0·66
Ca^{++}	1·05	0·99
F^-	1·02	1·36
Cl^-	1·21	1·81
O^-	1·11	1·40
S^-	1·29	1·84

a spherical shell of charge experiences no force from the shell. Hence the electrostatic restoring force is exerted by the fraction of the negative charge that is nearer to the centre than a, or in other words the charge $-Zea^3/R^3$. And that charge acts as if it were concentrated at the centre, according to the electrostatic result used already at the beginning of this chapter.

Coulomb's law may now be used to calculate the restoring force on the nuclear charge $+Ze$: the force has the magnitude

$$ka = (Ze) \cdot (Zea^3/R^3) \cdot (1/4\pi\epsilon_0 a^2).$$

Hence $k = (Ze)^2/4\pi\epsilon_0 R^3$, and a comparison of this expression with (3.4) yields the simple relation

$$\alpha = 4\pi\epsilon_0 R^3. \tag{3.5}$$

But the very simple form of (3.5) results from the simplicity of the assumptions used in deriving it. It is as applicable to an ion as to a neutral atom, even though the ion beams a net charge.

In order to decide how accurate it is, experimentally measured polarizabilities can be compared with experimentally measured sizes of ions. The polarizabilities are obtainable from interpretations of optical experiments; the sizes are obtainable from observations of how the ions pack together in crystals. As Table 3.2 shows, the rough calculation of polarizabilities turns out to be quite good. The measured polarizabilities of the listed ions increase roughly with the ionic volumes, but a little more slowly. Hence the agreement is better for small ions than for large.

These results can now be used to estimate the contribution made by polarization to the attractive energy in the ionic bond. Since the radii of

---

Discussion 3.4

DIPOLE–DIPOLE INTERACTION

In order to find the attractive energy of two dipoles that point in the same sense along their own direction, add the electrostatic energies of interaction of all the charge pairs within the dipoles:

$$E = \frac{q_1 q_2}{4\pi\epsilon_0}\left(\frac{1}{r} + \frac{1}{r+x_2-x_1} - \frac{1}{r-x_1} - \frac{1}{r+x_2}\right).$$

Expand each fraction in series, taking x_1 and x_2 small compared with r, and retaining only the first significant term in small quantities:

$$E = \frac{q_1 q_2}{4\pi\epsilon_0 r}\begin{bmatrix} 1 \\[4pt] +1 - \dfrac{x_2-x_1}{r} + \dfrac{(x_2-x_1)^2}{r^2} - \cdots \\[8pt] -1 - \dfrac{x_1}{r} - \dfrac{x_1^2}{r^2} - \cdots \\[8pt] -1 + \dfrac{x_2}{r} - \dfrac{x_2^2}{r^2} + \cdots \end{bmatrix}.$$

Thus $E \doteq -2(q_1 x_1)(q_2 x_2)/4\pi\epsilon_0 r^3 = -2\mu_1\mu_2/4\pi\epsilon_0 r^3$.

---

the ions are of the order 1 Å $= 10^{-10}$ m, the polarizabilities are of the order 10^{-40} F m^2.† An ion with one electronic charge (of magnitude $e = 1\cdot6 \times 10^{-19}$ C) establishes an electric field at a distance 2·5 Å (the typical interionic separation shown in Table 3.1) of the order $\mathbf{E} = e/4\pi\epsilon_0 r_0^2 \doteq 10^{10}$ V m^{-1}. Hence each ion induces in its partner a dipole (Fig. 3.3) whose moment is of the order $\mu = \alpha\mathbf{E} \doteq 10^{10} \times 10^{-40} = 10^{-30}$ C m.

As Discussion 3.4 shows, two dipoles of equal magnitude in the orientation shown in Fig. 3.3 have an interaction energy $-2\mu^2/4\pi\epsilon_0 r^3$. Substituting the magnitude of the dipole moment just calculated, and a typical value of r from Table 3.1, yields an interaction energy of about 0·13 eV. Thus the inclusion of polarization energy can remove some of the damage that the inclusion of repulsive energy worked on the agreement in Table 3.1. A third

---

† The electric field constant (permittivity of a vacuum) $\epsilon_0 = 8\cdot85 \times 10^{-12}$ F m^{-1}, so that $4\pi\epsilon_0 = 1\cdot11 \times 10^{-10}$ F m^{-1}.

important consideration in comparing these calculations with experimental results is suggested in Problem 3.2.

The foregoing discussion of their compressibility and distortability suggests that ions appear to be rigid only because the forces ordinarily encountered in our world are too feeble to affect them much. For many practical purposes the rigid-sphere model of an ion is remarkably useful. For example, ascribing to ions *effective radii*, which depend mostly on their species and little on their environment, proves to be a valuable guide in understanding the choice of crystal structure adopted by a large collection of oppositely charged ions.

PROBLEMS

3.1   Thermal agitation causes an alkali halide molecule to vibrate about its equilibrium length r_0. Since it is then an oscillating dipole, it can interact with electromagnetic radiation. Use (3.1) and the results of Discussion 3.2 to calculate the vibration frequency of the sodium chloride molecule. In what range of the electromagnetic spectrum does this frequency lie?

3.2   Quantum mechanics has shown that any harmonic oscillator retains a minimum vibrational energy $\frac{1}{2}hv$, where v is its frequency and h is Planck's constant ($6 \cdot 62 \times 10^{-34}$ J s). Hence, even when it is not thermally excited, an alkali halide molecule must have an energy higher (less negative) than the energies calculated in this chapter, by the amount of this so-called *zero-point energy*. Calculate the magnitude of that zero-point energy, using the frequency calculated in Problem 3.1. By taking it into account, do you better or worsen the agreement of the calculated with the experimental dissociation energy?

4. Dispersion Forces

THE rare gases such as neon and argon are remarkably inert: they do not form ionic bonds, and they show little tendency to share electrons with other atoms to form covalent bonds. Hence at first glance one might expect to find no attractive force between the atoms, but only a repulsive force when they come close to one another. As a matter of experimental fact, however, the atoms do attract one another weakly when they are near together, though still far enough apart so that repulsive forces do not dominate the interaction.

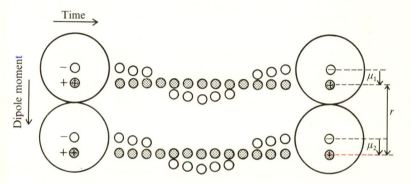

FIG. 4.1. A pair of dipoles, oscillating in phase in two atoms, could attract each other at all times. But the dipoles in adjacent atoms are not so closely correlated.

In order to understand these weak forces, it is well to remember that the electrons are not actually stationary charge clouds around the nuclei but rapidly moving swarms of negatively charged particles. On the average the centre of mass, and therefore the centre of charge, of the electrons is at the position of the nucleus about which they swarm; but instantaneously it is not, and the atom has a rapidly fluctuating dipole moment. It might seem at first that this cannot lead to attraction between the two atoms because the average dipole moment of each is zero. But if the oscillations of the dipole moments of the two atoms are correlated in phase, an attractive force can arise, as Fig. 4.1 suggests.

This figure portrays the instantaneous dipole moments of two neighbouring atoms, varying with time and perfectly correlated in phase, so that they attract each other maximally at all times. A glance at Discussion 3.4 makes clear that in that case the energy of the system would be lowered by the amount $2\mu_1\mu_2/4\pi\epsilon_0 r^3$ averaged over time. It is tempting to argue that, since a system tries to readjust itself into a condition of minimum energy, the correlation will be perfect. But the electrons are subjected within the atoms to other influences, and some are much stronger than this weak interaction between the two atoms.

Then how closely can these oscillating dipoles correlate their phases? There are several ways of answering this question, all of which give results that are at least qualitatively consistent.

The simplest way is to think of the fluctuating dipole in one atom as establishing a fluctuating electric field at the second atom. Then, using the results of the discussion of polarizability in the last chapter, one can conclude

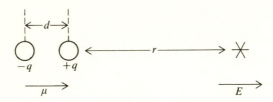

FIG. 4.2. The electric field due to a dipole, at a distance r along its direction, is the field due to the two charges that form the dipole. By a procedure like that of Discussion 3.4, $\mathbf{E} = q/4\pi\epsilon_0[1/r^2 - 1/(r+d)^2] \doteq 2qd/4\pi\epsilon_0 r^3 = 2\mu/4\pi\epsilon_0 r^3$. Notice that, by convention, the vector representing a dipole moment points from its negative toward its positive charge.

that the magnitude of the correlated dipole in the second atom will be the product of the polarizability of the second atom times the electric field due to the dipole in the first atom.

To pursue this calculation, notice that the field due to a dipole of moment μ_1, at a distance r along its direction, is $2\mu_1/4\pi\epsilon_0 r^3$ (Fig. 4.2). If the polarizability of the second atom is α, the induced dipole has a moment given by $\mu_2 = 2\alpha\mu_1/4\pi\epsilon_0 r^3$. Hence the potential energy of the combination of the induced dipole and the original dipole is $-2\mu_1\mu_2/4\pi\epsilon_0 r^3 = -\alpha\mu_1^2/4\pi^2\epsilon_0^2 r^6$. Although μ_1 is fluctuating, and its average value is zero, μ_1^2 is positive: the value of μ_1^2 averaged over time is the relevant quantity to use in this expression for the potential energy.

Two results of this simple analysis are important. In the first place, the potential energy function for this interaction varies as $1/r^6$. It falls off very rapidly as the distance between the atoms increases; the force, falling off as $1/r^7$,† is a short-range force in contrast with the attraction between two ions, which falls off as $1/r^2$. In the second place, the force is larger the larger the polarizability of the atom.

† Recall that the force, tending to increase the value of a coordinate in a mechanical system, varies as the negative of the derivative of the potential energy of the system with respect to the coordinate.

But it is hard to find any method for calculating the average value of μ_1^2, and so to find the order of magnitude of the force. For this reason, and in order to improve confidence in the quantitative relations that the model proposes between this force and the polarizability and interatomic separation, it is useful to look at an alternative method of handling the problem.

In the second method the fluctuating dipoles of the two atoms are treated as a pair of oscillators that are weakly coupled by their interaction. The method is more satisfying in two respects. It deals with the two atoms on the same footing at the outset, instead of focussing attention on one of them.

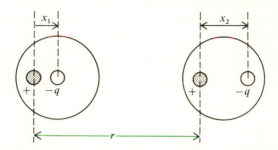

Fig. 4.3. In the coupled-oscillator model of two atoms interacting with the dispersion force, a portion of the negative charge cloud in each atom is instantaneously displaced from the nucleus, to give the atoms instantaneous dipole moments of magnitudes qx_1 and qx_2.

Furthermore it leads more naturally to the interpretation of its results in terms of measurable properties of the atoms.

Imagine two atoms that are identical, and that possess oscillating dipoles in each of which the centre of positive charge stays fixed. The centre of negative charge oscillates back and forth along the line joining the positive charges so that the instantaneous displacements of each from the centres of positive charge are such as those denoted by x_1 and x_2 in Fig. 4.3. As in the study of polarizability in the last chapter, there is a force, proportional to the displacement, tending to restore the cloud of negative charge in each atom to the zero position; and again the force constant k can be related to the polarizability α of the atom.

Now simplify the picture of the fluctuating dipole moment of each atom into a simple harmonic oscillator, with the force constant k, whose mass m is the mass of the moving cloud of electrons. The natural frequency of the oscillator in each of the atoms is then

$$v_0 = \frac{1}{2\pi}\sqrt{\left(\frac{k}{m}\right)}. \tag{4.1}$$

But when the atoms approach each other, the electrostatic interactions between the dipoles provide a weak coupling between them. The dipoles then behave like all other coupled oscillators: the coupling endows them with two distinct normal modes of vibration whose frequencies differ from v_0 by amounts that increase as the coupling increases. In this case one frequency is higher and the other is lower than v_0.

Assuming that each oscillator is in its ground state before it is coupled, you can take the energy of the uncoupled system as $2(\frac{1}{2}hv_0)$. Then when the system is coupled, its energy can be taken as $\frac{1}{2}hv_1 + \frac{1}{2}hv_2$, where v_1 and v_2 are the frequencies associated with the two normal modes of vibration. Since the average value of v_1 and v_2 is slightly lower than v_0, the energy of the system is lowered by the coupling.

The details of the suggested calculation are shown in an appendix to this chapter. It leads to a calculated frequency

$$v_0 = \frac{q}{2\pi} \sqrt{\left(\frac{1}{m\alpha}\right)}, \qquad (4.2)$$

and a binding energy

$$\Delta E = \frac{3hq}{128\pi^3 \epsilon_0^2 r^6} \sqrt{\left(\frac{\alpha^3}{m}\right)}, \qquad (4.3)$$

where h is Planck's constant, and q and m are the charge and mass of the oscillating charge-cloud.

It remains to decide what are reasonable values of q and m to use in this expression: what charge moves in the oscillator and what mass is associated with that charge. The calculated energy turns out to agree best with the observed energy when one assumes that only those electrons in the atom that are least tightly bound to the nucleus, those in the outermost shell, will readily suffer distortion of their states, and thus will make the major contributions to the oscillation. If there are N electrons in the outermost shell, $q = Ne_0$ and $m = Nm_0$, where e_0 and m_0 are the charge and mass of the electron. Then (4.3) can be written

$$\Delta E = \frac{3he_0}{128\pi^3 \epsilon_0^2 r^6} \sqrt{\left(\frac{N\alpha^3}{m_0}\right)}. \qquad (4.4)$$

For convenience in practical calculation, it is helpful to rewrite this equation by making use of the facts that an atomic polarizability is of the order 10^{-40} F m^2, and an interatomic distance is of the order 10^{-10} m. Let r' and α' represent distance and polarizability in these more natural atomic units. The equation then becomes

$$\Delta E = \frac{1 \cdot 26 \times 10^{-18}}{(r')^6} \sqrt{\{N(\alpha')^3\}} \text{ joules.}$$

Now check this result by calculating the binding energy of solid argon, and comparing the calculated value with that determined by experiments in which the heat required to vaporize argon is measured, and thermodynamic considerations are used to correct for the work done by the vapour in pushing against its environment, and thus to derive an 'experimental' binding energy. Such a calculation proceeds by finding first the energy in a single bond between two argon atoms, and then multiplying that energy by the number of bonds in the solid. Since the dispersion force falls off so rapidly with increasing distance, only the bonds between the nearest neighbours need be considered.

In solid argon the distance between nearest neighbours is 3·84 Å. The polarizability of an argon atom is $1·85 \times 10^{-40}$ F m^2, and there are eight electrons in its outer shell. With $N = 8$, and $\alpha' = 1·85$, and $r' = 3·84$, the equation yields $\Delta E = 2·4 \times 10^{-21}$ J, or 0·015 eV. It is interesting to notice that the ionic bond in a molecule of an alkali halide, if the ions were separated

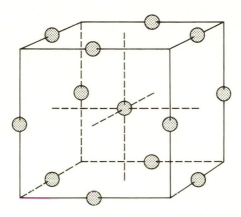

FIG. 4.4. In solid argon each atom is surrounded by twelve others at the same distance.

by the same distance, would have approximately the bonding energy $e_0^2/4\pi\epsilon_0 r = 3·7$ eV—more than two hundred times larger.

Argon crystallizes in a close-packed structure (Fig. 4.4) giving each atom twelve nearest neighbours at the same distance. Since each nearest-neighbour bond is shared between two atoms, the number of bonds per atom in the solid is six. Thus the binding energy per atom of the solid is six times the energy per bond. The calculated energy, 0·09 eV, agrees well with the experimental value.

But your satisfaction with this agreement may be less when you recall that our calculation has still left out the repulsive energy—the energy due to the repulsive force that balances the attractive force between the atoms and holds them at a fixed distance. The preceding chapter showed that the repulsive energy reduces the calculated binding energy in the ionic bond of an alkali halide molecule by about 10 per cent. In the ionic bond the attractive force has a long range, whereas the repulsive force has a short range. But in the present case the two forces that balance each other are both of short range, and it becomes even more important to include the energies due to both, as Problem 4.4 suggests.

Another way to obtain an approximate relationship between the dispersion force and other properties of an atom is to relate the frequency v_0 of the oscillating dipole to some quantity that can be determined experimentally. The following crude argument, for example, makes it seem reasonable to relate that frequency to the *first ionization energy* of the atom.

If the atomic dipole behaved in a classical fashion, it could be driven by an applied electromagnetic force. If the applied force oscillated with the

TABLE 4.1   *Binding energies of neutral molecules*

	Ionization Energy (Electron Volts)	Polarizability (F m$^2 \times 10^{40}$)	Binding Energy (Electron Volts per Molecule)	
			Calculated	Observed
Ne	21·5	0·45	0·017	0·026
A	15·7	1·85	0·078	0·088
Kr	14·0	2·83	0·135	0·122
N_2	15·8	1·94	0·070	0·081
O_2	11·2	1·75	0·064	0·090
Cl_2	18·2	5·12	0·312	0·323
CH_4	14·5	2·87	0·107	0·117

frequency of the oscillating dipole, the dipole would resonate. If it resonated strongly, the amplitude of its oscillation might increase sufficiently to shake an electron out of the atom.

Now in fact light can ionize atoms, if each photon of the light has sufficient energy to contribute the ionization energy. Each photon of light whose frequency is v carries the energy hv, where h is Planck's constant. These facts suggest that the ionization energy I of an atom be set equal to hv_0, where v_0 is the frequency of its oscillating dipole.

By substituting I for hv_0 in the equation $\Delta E = 3hv_0\alpha^2/64\pi^2\epsilon_0^2 r^6$, derived in the appendix, one obtains

$$\Delta E = \frac{3\alpha^2}{64\pi^2\epsilon_0^2 r^6}\, I. \tag{4.5}$$

It turns out that binding energies calculated from this equation agree quite well with experimental values, not only for atoms but for neutral molecules that have no fixed dipole moments, such as nitrogen and methane. More because of experimental agreement than because of the shaky argument lying behind it, the equation is often used to make estimates of dispersion energies. Table 4.1 shows the relevant quantities for several solid substances.

These successes give confidence in calculating the contributions of dispersion forces to the binding energies of materials in which the principal binding forces have other origins.

Calculation of energies due to dispersion forces explains also the binding energies of the solid hydrogen halides, shown in Table 4.2. The molecules of HCl, HBr, and HI have permanent dipoles, and their dipole moments decrease in that order. If the binding forces in crystals of these compounds came primarily from the interaction of the permanent dipole moments, the binding energies should decrease also in that order, whereas in fact they increase.

TABLE 4.2   *Binding energies of hydrogen halides*

	Dipole Moment (C m $\times 10^{30}$)	Polarizability (F m$^2 \times 10^{40}$)	Binding Energy (Electron Volts per Molecule)	
			Calculated	Observed
HCl	3·57	2·93	0·176	0·220
HBr	2·60	3·98	0·197	0·240
HI	1·27	6·00	0·291	0·270

But other evidence has shown that, above certain critical temperatures characteristic for each compound, the molecules in these solids are rotating rapidly end for end. Time-average interaction of their permanent dipole moments can be no larger than the correlation of these rotations permits. As the temperature increases, that correlation decreases; it is negligible at their vapourization temperatures. Their heats of vapourization depend on the energies due to dispersion forces, which have the proper sequence to explain the observations on these materials.

APPENDIX

A COUPLED-OSCILLATOR MODEL FOR THE DISPERSION FORCE

A harmonic oscillator of force constant k and mass m has potential energy $\frac{1}{2}kx^2$ and kinetic energy $p^2/2m$, where x and p are its instantaneous displacement and momentum, and it oscillates with a frequency $v_0 = 1/2\pi\sqrt{(k/m)}$. Thus the kinetic energy of the system of Fig. 4.1 is

$$U_{\text{kin}} = \frac{1}{2m}(p_1^2 + p_2^2) \qquad (A4.1)$$

and the potential energy is

$$U_{\text{pot}} = \frac{1}{2}kx_1^2 + \frac{1}{2}kx_2^2 - 2\frac{q^2 x_1 x_2}{4\pi\epsilon_0 r^3}, \qquad (A4.2)$$

where the last term is the instantaneous energy of their coupling as Fig. 4.1 describes.

The study of this system is facilitated by an elementary application of the method of normal coordinates.† In this case the normal coordinates x'_1 and x'_2 are given by

$$x_1 = \frac{1}{\sqrt{2}}(x'_1 + x'_2), \quad \text{whence} \quad p_1 = \frac{1}{\sqrt{2}}(p'_1 + p'_2);$$

$$x_2 = \frac{1}{\sqrt{2}}(x'_1 - x'_2), \quad \text{whence} \quad p_2 = \frac{1}{\sqrt{2}}(p'_1 - p'_2).$$

(A4.3)

By substitution from (A4.3), (A4.1) and (A4.2) become

$$U_{\text{kin}} = \frac{1}{2m}(p'^2_1 + p'^2_2),$$

$$U_{\text{pot}} = \frac{1}{2}\left(k - \frac{2q^2}{4\pi\epsilon_0 r^3}\right)x'^2_1 + \frac{1}{2}\left(k + \frac{2q^2}{4\pi\epsilon_0 r^3}\right)x'^2_2.$$

(A4.4)

These correspond to the kinetic and potential energies of two uncoupled oscillators with the force constants

$$k_1 = k - \frac{2q^2}{4\pi\epsilon_0 r^3}, \qquad k_2 = k + \frac{2q^2}{4\pi\epsilon_0 r^3}.$$

(A4.5)

Hence the frequencies of these oscillators are

$$\nu_1 = \frac{1}{2\pi}\sqrt{\left\{\frac{1}{m}\left(k - \frac{2q^2}{4\pi\epsilon_0 r^3}\right)\right\}},$$

$$\nu_2 = \frac{1}{2\pi}\sqrt{\left\{\frac{1}{m}\left(k + \frac{2q^2}{4\pi\epsilon_0 r^3}\right)\right\}}.$$

(A4.6)

Now the zero-point energy of the two uncoupled oscillators‡ is

$$E = \tfrac{1}{2}h\nu_0 + \tfrac{1}{2}h\nu_0 = h\nu_0.$$

(A4.7)

Similarly, the zero-point energy of the two coupled oscillators is

$$E' = \tfrac{1}{2}h\nu_1 + \tfrac{1}{2}h\nu_2.$$

(A4.8)

Since the coupling is weak, the quantity $2q^2/4\pi\epsilon_0 r^3$ must be small compared to k. Then the value of (A4.8) can be found by expanding the expressions (A4.6) in power series in $2q^2/4\pi\epsilon_0 k r^3$. Use of the series expansions

$$\sqrt{(1 \pm a)} = 1 \pm \frac{a}{2} - \frac{a^2}{8} \pm \frac{a^3}{16} - \dots,$$

(A4.9)

yields the new zero-point energy

$$E' = h\nu_0\left(1 - \frac{q^4}{32\pi^2\epsilon_0^2 k^2 r^6} - \dots\right).$$

(A4.10)

† In many mechanical systems the potential energy is expressible as a quadratic form, containing cross-products, in the coordinates; and the kinetic energy is expressible as a sum of squares of the conjugate momenta. It is then always possible, and it is usually advantageous, to make a linear transformation of the coordinates, such that the potential energy becomes a sum of the squares of the new coordinates and the kinetic energy is still a sum of the squares of the new conjugate momenta. Important examples appear in elastic theory and in the theory of specific heats.

‡ See *Stationary states*, Chapter 5.

Thus the energy of the coupled system is less than that of the uncoupled system by approximately the value of the second term in the bracket:

$$\Delta E = h v_0 \frac{q^4}{32 \pi^2 \epsilon_0^2 k^2 r^6}. \tag{A4.11}$$

A somewhat more careful analysis, in which the oscillations are not restricted to the line of centres of the atoms but can occur in any direction in space, changes the numerical factor in (A4.11) from $\frac{1}{32}$ to $\frac{3}{64}$:

$$\Delta E = h v_0 \frac{3 q^4}{64 \pi^2 \epsilon_0^2 k^2 r^6}. \tag{A4.12}$$

The force constant k is related to the polarizability by $k = q^2/\alpha$, as the last chapter showed. Hence (A4.12) becomes

$$\Delta E = \frac{3 h v_0 \alpha^2}{64 \pi^2 \epsilon_0^2 r^6}. \tag{A4.13}$$

Moreover that value of k can be used in the expression for the frequency, to give

$$v_0 = \frac{q}{2\pi} \sqrt{\left(\frac{1}{m\alpha}\right)}, \tag{A4.14}$$

and thus the dispersion energy

$$\Delta E = \frac{3h}{128 \pi^3 \epsilon_0^2 r^6} \sqrt{\left(\frac{q^2 \alpha^3}{m}\right)}. \tag{A4.15}$$

PROBLEMS

4.1 The tetrahedral molecules of methane, CH_4, are in rotation over much of the temperature range in which methane is solid, and you can regard the solid as made of spheres of radius 2·18 Å, having the same arrangement as that of the atoms in solid argon.
(a) Verify approximately the calculated value of the binding energy shown in Table 4.1.
(b) What 'number of electrons' in (4.4) would give the same result?

4.2 The carbon monoxide molecule is isoelectronic and isobaric with the nitrogen molecule, and has a very small dipole moment. The densities of the solid forms of the two are nearly the same. Assuming that they have the same crystal structure, calculate a value of the binding energy of solid carbon monoxide from that of nitrogen (Table 4.1) for comparison with the experimental value 2·09 kcal per mole. The polarizability of a CO molecule is $2\cdot21 \times 10^{-40}$ F m^2, and its ionization potential is 329 kcal per mole.

4.3 The relative density of solid argon is 1·7 and of solid krypton is 3·2, and both adopt the same crystal structure. From these data, the atomic weights, and the data for polarizabilities and ionization potentials in Table 4.1 calculate the binding energy of krypton from that of argon shown in Table 4.1.

4.4 In a more refined calculation than that of the text, the binding energy of crystals held together by dispersion forces must include the repulsive contribution that keeps the atoms apart. For this purpose an expression similar to that in Chapter 3, (3.1), for ionic crystals can be used. The most convenient is the so-called 'Lennard-Jones' or '6–12' potential:

$$U = -\frac{A}{a^6} + \frac{B}{a^{12}},$$

where A and B are constants and a is some characteristic distance in the crystal, such as the nearest-neighbour distance.

(a) If U is the binding energy per mole, what is A for a crystal of atoms of polarizability α and ionization potential I when you take a as the nearest-neighbour distance, consider only nearest-neighbour interactions, and give each atom twelve nearest neighbours.

(b) Find B in terms of A and the equilibrium separation a, and hence 'correct' the calculated value for the binding energy of argon obtained in the text.

(c) Noticing that the calculated value (b) is now smaller than the experimental value, and that the calculation is quite sensitive to your choice of the exponent for the repulsive potential and also to your choice of the number N of participating electrons, recalculate the binding energy of solid argon by assuming that all the electrons in each atom (atomic number = 18) contribute, and correct your calculation by using the potential $U = -A/a^6 + B/a^{18}$.

5. The Simplest Molecule

So far the discussion of the attractions between atoms has been able to proceed with little recourse to the quantum-mechanical description of the behaviour of the electrons forming the bonds. By accepting the fact that a sodium atom will tend to lose an electron, and a chlorine atom to gain one, it was possible to examine the bond between the resulting ions by using classical electrostatic ideas. By accepting the fact that the electrons in an atom behave somewhat like a distortable charge-cloud around its nucleus, similar ideas availed in examining the dispersion force between two neutral atoms. Relatively simple arguments have made the picture of electrostatic bonding quantitatively reasonable, both for ions and for uncharged atoms.

Any examination of the *covalent bond*, however, comes face to face with the detailed behaviour of the electrons that form the bond, and thus with the wave mechanics necessary to describe that behaviour. There is much flexibility in the behaviour, as the chemical diversity of our world mutely testifies. Chemists have found many rules to help predict and describe the occurrence and character of covalent bonds between the various atomic species, and their science continues to make new discoveries and new formulations.

Instead of detailing their methods and results, the next few chapters will search more physically for the dynamical behaviour that enables electrons to form covalent bonds between atoms. We inquire when nuclei and electrons form a stable system in which the nuclei lie close to one another. The cases chosen for examination are the simplest, and they are made even simpler by representing them by plausible models. This chapter in particular will carry that procedure almost to absurdity: its models, though plausible, will be wrong. Often an examination of a plausible idea that turns out to be wrong helps to make clear what is right.

Characteristically a covalent bond between two atoms is an *electron-pair bond*; two electrons of opposite spin are in states described by wave functions that have the same shape. But a bond formed by only one electron has most of the same physical characteristics. Look first, therefore, at a *one-electron bond*, in particular at the simplest instance of it, the hydrogen-molecule ion H_2^+.

The hydrogen-molecule ion, composed of two protons, each with charge $+e$, and one electron with charge $-e$, is an observable species of matter. There are good experimental values of the average separation of the two protons in the ground state of the molecule—the bond length R_0— and of the (negative) energy of the molecule in that state relative to a zero of energy in which the two protons and the electron are all far from one another and at rest—the binding energy U_0.†

It is easy to guess roughly what the behaviour of this system will be. If the protons are anywhere near each other, the electron will be attracted by both protons and will describe some orbit about them. The protons, each with a mass 1840 times the mass of the electron, will be relatively sluggish in responding to the pull of the rapidly moving electron. But if the electron spends more time between than away from them, it will pull them toward each other on the average. As they approach each other, their positive charges will repel each other more and more, and furthermore the electron

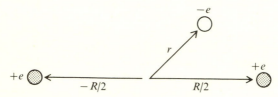

FIG. 5.1. The hydrogen-molecule ion contains two protons and one electron. In a coordinate system whose origin is at the mid-point between the nuclei, the instantaneous potential energy of the electron at any point r, in the field of the nuclei at $\pm R/2$, is expressed by

$$V(\mathbf{r}) = -e^2/4\pi\epsilon_0 \, |\mathbf{r} - \mathbf{R}/2| - e^2/4\pi\epsilon_0 \, |\mathbf{r} + \mathbf{R}/2|.$$

will have less and less space between them in which to spend time. For both these reasons the protons will find some separation R_0 at which these competing effects balance.

To examine this system exactly, however, offers a problem in the dynamics of three charged particles interacting according to Coulomb's law (Fig. 5.1), an instance of the famous *three-body problem*. Even in classical mechanics, to say nothing of wave mechanics, it has not been solved analytically. The first approximation to introduce is suggested by the expectation that the relatively heavy protons will move so much less rapidly than the electron that they will be responding primarily to a cloud of electronic charge.

In pursuing this suggestion, one would first determine what the total energy of the system would be if the protons were somehow held fixed at an arbitrary separation R. That energy will have three parts: the electrostatic repulsive energy of the fixed nuclei, the average kinetic energy of the moving electron, and the average potential energy of the electron in the electrostatic field of the fixed nuclei. Their sum will be $U(R)$, a function of R.

Then $U(R)$ can be used to determine the motions of the protons by thinking of it as furnishing the potential energy of the proton pair at the separation R.

† *Binding energy* is a term used somewhat loosely, and this monograph is no exception. In this chapter it will mean the energy required to disperse the electrons and nuclei to great distances, and will be distinguished from the *dissociation energy* required to disperse the ingredients of a molecule or a crystal into widely separated atoms or ions.

If $U(R)$ has a minimum at some value of R, that value of R is the R_0 sought,[†] and that value of U is U_0, and the system can be expected to oscillate about the separation R_0.[‡]

Thus the electronic part of the present three-body problem is reduced to a one-body problem. But the function $U(R)$ for the hydrogen-molecule ion still cannot be expressed in closed form in terms of well-known tabulated functions: its values must be obtained by numerical integration of a differential equation. More insight into the three contributions to $U(R)$ comes from examining simplified models.

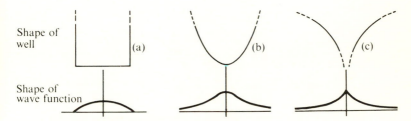

Fig. 5.2. In a potential well with a single minimum, the wave function for the ground state has a single maximum. The wells above are for (a) the one-dimensional box, (b) the one-dimensional harmonic oscillator, and (c) an atom, in cross-section.

The first contribution, the potential energy of the nuclei, is clearly

$$U_{\text{nuc}} = \frac{e^2}{4\pi\epsilon_0 R}. \tag{5.1}$$

To find the contributions of the kinetic and potential energies of the electron, begin by lumping them together. The electron is assumed to be bound by a *potential well*. Its state is assumed to be the ground state described by solving Schrödinger's equation. The energy $E(R)$ of that state is the total energy—kinetic plus potential—of the electron, and hence

$$U(R) = E(R) + \frac{e^2}{4\pi\epsilon_0 R}. \tag{5.2}$$

In order to picture what the ground state might look like, compare this potential well with some others, shown in Fig. 5.2, that are simpler: (a) the square well, (b) the parabolic well, and (c) the well offered to an electron by a single nucleus. The wave functions for the ground state of a particle in all

† The notation R_0 for the interatomic separation here replaces the earlier notation r_0 because of the use of r for the coordinate of the electron.

‡ This method of dividing up problems in the behaviour of systems of electrons and nuclei, called the 'Born–Oppenheimer approximation', was introduced by Max Born and J. R. Oppenheimer, working together in Göttingen in 1927.

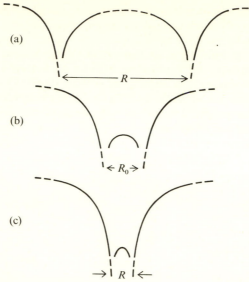

FIG. 5.3. The potential well, shown in cross-section for the electron in the hydrogen-molecule ion, has two minima. As the distance R between the nuclei decreases, the well approaches more nearly the single well offered by a single nucleus.

these wells have a roughly similar form: all reach a maximum at the middle of the well.†

The shape of the potential well offered to an electron by two nuclei depends, of course, on the distance between the nuclei. As Fig. 5.3 shows, the nuclei offer two wells, each quite like Fig. 5.2(c) when they are far apart (a), and one well of the same sort when they are very close together (c). At an intermediate distance (b) the well looks roughly like a box with walls of finite height.

That comparison suggests the following crude approximation to the facts. Assume that the average potential energy of the electron will be roughly that

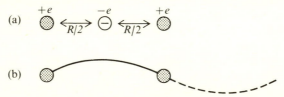

FIG. 5.4. A suggested approximation (a) for the average potential energy of the electron in a hydrogen-molecule ion places the electron midway between the nuclei, and (b) for the average kinetic energy uses a de Broglie wavelength of twice the distance between the nuclei.

† The wave functions for some of these wells are discussed in *Stationary states*, Chapters 3 and 5, and in *The nature of atoms*.

of an electron at rest midway between the nuclei; and assume that the average kinetic energy of the electron will be roughly that of a free particle whose de Broglie wavelength λ is twice the distance between the nuclei. Fig. 5.4 pictures the two ingredients of this guess. As Fig. 5.5 shows, the guess corresponds to a one-dimensional model. In that model the electron is in a one-dimensional box whose bottom represents the electron's potential energy when it is midway between the nuclei, and whose sides confine the electron to the line between the nuclei. Of course guessing that the box width should be the same as the nuclear separation is only a guess. Furthermore, there are differences in the ground-state energies of one-dimensional and three-dimensional wells. But the energy and separation calculated for this model

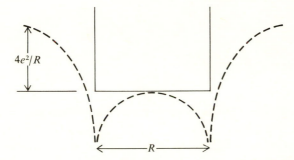

Fig. 5.5. Using the one-dimensional model of the hydrogen-molecule ion shown in Fig. 5.4 is equivalent to thinking of the electron as in a box whose width R is the same as the separation of the protons.

turn out to have the right order of magnitude, and some useful insights come from studying it.

The appropriate calculations for this model are carried out in Discussion 5.1. The electronic potential energy goes down as $1/R$, just as the ionic potential energy does in the calculations for the ionic bond in Chapter 3. The electronic kinetic energy goes up as $1/R^2$, behaving somewhat like the repulsive energy in Chapter 3. Thus, as in that earlier work, the energy passes through a minimum as R varies. In this case the minimum yields the values $R_0 = 1.74$ Å and $U_0 = -12.3$ eV. Since the experimental values for the hydrogen-molecule ion are $R_0 = 1.06$ Å and $U_0 = -16.3$ eV, the agreement is rather good for so crude a model.†

But you can easily get from this model a misconception of the roles that the three ingredients of $U(R)$ play in the actual case. In the model there is a minimum in $U(R)$ only because the electronic kinetic energy increases more rapidly at small R than the total potential energy of the electron and the

† The agreement becomes less impressive on comparing the *dissociation energies*—the energy of the molecule-ion relative to the energy of a hydrogen atom and a proton separated from each other—as Problem 5.1 shows.

Discussion 5.1

A SIMPLE MODEL OF A ONE-ELECTRON BOND

If the wavelength of the electron is $\lambda = 2R$ (Fig. 5.4(b)), the de Broglie relation for the momentum, $p = h/\lambda$, gives $p = h/2R$ and thus the kinetic energy

$$U_{\text{kin}} = \frac{p^2}{2m} = \frac{h^2}{8mR^2}. \tag{D5.1}$$

If the electronic potential energy is as represented in Fig. 5.4(a),

$$U_{\text{pot}} = \frac{1}{4\pi\epsilon_0}\left(\frac{-e^2}{R/2} - \frac{e^2}{R/2}\right) = \frac{-e^2}{\pi\epsilon_0 R}. \tag{D5.2}$$

Hence the total electronic energy is

$$E(R) = U_{\text{kin}} + U_{\text{pot}} = \frac{h^2}{8mR^2} - \frac{e^2}{\pi\epsilon_0 R}, \tag{D5.3}$$

and the total energy of the system (neglecting any kinetic energy of vibration of the nuclei) is

$$U(R) = \frac{h^2}{8mR^2} - \frac{3e^2}{4\pi\epsilon_0 R}. \tag{D5.4}$$

By differentiating $U(R)$ with respect to R, a minimum is found at

$$\frac{-h^2}{4mR_0^3} + \frac{3e^2}{4\pi\epsilon_0 R_0^2} = 0, \quad \text{or} \quad R_0 = \frac{4\pi\epsilon_0 h^2}{12me^2}. \tag{D5.5}$$

At this value of R_0, (D5.4) yields

$$U_0 = -\frac{9me^4}{8\pi^2\epsilon_0^2 h^2}. \tag{D5.6}$$

When the values

$$h = 6.62 \times 10^{-34} \text{ J s},$$
$$e = -1.60 \times 10^{-19} \text{ C},$$
$$m = 9.11 \times 10^{-31} \text{ kg},$$

are put into (D5.5) and (D5.6), they yield the values

$$R_0 = 1.74 \text{ Å}, \qquad U_0 = -12.3 \text{ eV},$$

to be compared with the experimental values, 1.06 Å and -16.3 eV.

---

nuclei decreases. Hence in the model the factor that keeps the nuclei apart is the electronic kinetic energy.

In the real case, Fig. 5.3 shows that the electronic kinetic energy cannot increase in that way. As the nuclei get very close to each other, the electron sees a pair of charges that more and more closely resembles the double charge on a helium nucleus. The only reason that the electronic kinetic energy increases indefinitely in the model is because the model requires the electron to stay in a box (Fig. 5.5) that becomes indefinitely small.

In the real molecule the electron is not in such a box. As the nuclei approach each other, the electron spends more and more time to the left of the nucleus on the left and to the right of the nucleus on the right. Thus as the internuclear distance shortens, the wavelength of the electron does not decrease as much, and its kinetic energy does not increase as much, as the model suggests. And since the electron spends more and more time away from the position midway between the nuclei, its potential energy does not go down as fast in fact as in the model.

Indeed, examining the two extremes shown in Fig. 5.3(a) and (c) makes clear that, when the nuclei are far apart (a), the total electronic energy will be that of the hydrogen atom, for the electron will be on one nucleus or the other; and when the nuclei coincide (c), the total electronic energy will be that of the helium ion, He^+. Since the energy of an electron in the ground state of a one-electron atom varies as $-Z^2$, where Z is the atomic number of the atom, the total electronic energy $E(R)$ must go down smoothly by a factor of 4 as R decreases from $R = \infty$ to $R = 0$. Clearly what finally keeps the nuclei apart in the hydrogen-molecule ion must be their electrostatic repulsion U_{nuc}, not the electronic kinetic energy. The calculated model yields an approximation to the correct internuclear distance and binding energy only by good fortune.

Since this model has the major defect of confining the electron too closely to the space between the nuclei, consider another one-dimensional model which avoids this defect, a 'delta-well model'. A 'delta well'—a well that is infinitesimally wide but infinitely deep—affords one bound state for a particle.† As the width l of the well approaches zero, and the potential energy V of a particle in the well becomes negatively infinite, in such a way that the product $Vl = -\eta$ remains finite, then the energy of the electron in the bound state takes the form $-E = \eta^2/4$, and its wave function to the left and the right of the well is

$$\psi_l = Ae^{\eta x/2}, \qquad \psi_r = Ae^{-\eta x/2}. \tag{5.3}$$

Thus the wave function for an electron in the presence of the well looks like Fig. 5.6: it has the same form as a one-dimensional cross-section of the wave function for the ground state of the hydrogen atom. This correspondence suggests using two such wells to make a one-dimensional model for examining the ground state of the hydrogen-molecule ion.

The model is simple enough for exact calculation: an appendix to this chapter carries out the formalities, finding two different possible states for the electron. In one state the wave function is symmetrical about the midpoint between the two wells, and in the other state the wave function is antisymmetrical, as Fig. 5.7 shows. The energy of a particle in either of these states approaches the same value as the distance between the nuclei becomes very

† The properties of a particle in the presence of a delta well are examined in *The nature of atoms*, Chapter 4.

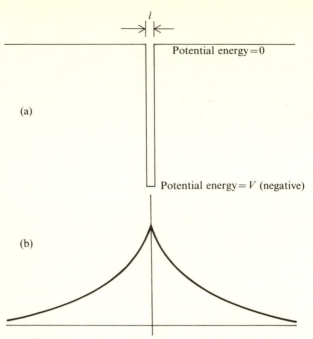

Fig. 5.6. In the 'delta well' (a) the potential energy falls abruptly to a large negative value of V over a tiny distance l; and V is allowed to become infinite and l to vanish in such a way that the product Vl has the finite value of $-\eta$. The well affords one bound state for a particle, whose wave function (b) has the shape of a cross-section of the wave function for the ground state of an electron in an atom. Increasing the value of the single parameter η that characterizes the well is equivalent to increasing the positive charge of the nucleus of an atom.

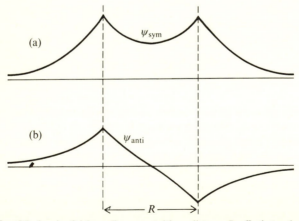

Fig. 5.7. A pair of delta wells, separated by a distance R, affords two bound states for a particle, whose wave functions are, respectively, symmetrical and antisymmetrical about the midpoint between the wells.

large. For an electron whose wave function has the symmetrical form, the energy decreases in the expected way from that of the hydrogen atom to that of the helium atom as the nuclei come together. For the antisymmetrical wave function, however, the corresponding energy increases as the separation between the nuclei is reduced. These energies are plotted as functions of R in Fig. 5.8.

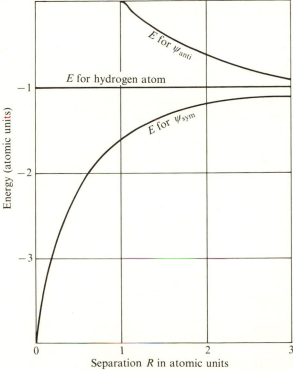

FIG. 5.8. The energies of an electron in the two states afforded by two delta wells, as functions of the distance between the wells.

Notice a rough analogy between what is happening here and what happens to two harmonic oscillators that are coupled by a weak spring, described in the last chapter. When the nuclei are far apart, the two electronic states are analogous to two identical oscillators that are uncoupled. Each nucleus affords a bound state for the electron; the two states are identical except that they are located in two different places, and both wave functions give the electron an even chance of being at either nucleus. When the nuclei are infinitely separated, the squares of the symmetrical and antisymmetrical wave functions will be the same, and thus give the same probability distribution for the electron. As the nuclei come closer to each other, the energy level is split, in a way similar to the splitting described in the last chapter for the frequencies of the two identical oscillators when they are coupled. You may find it helpful to think of the two identical states, afforded by the nuclei, as coupled, and thus providing two states with properties that differ increasingly as the coupling is increased by decreasing the nuclear separation.

Clearly an electron whose wave function has the antisymmetrical form cannot provide a stable bond for the molecule, for both the electronic and the nuclear repulsive energies increase monotonically with decreasing nuclear separation. An electron in the symmetrical wave function might give bonding, since $E(R)$ decreases monotonically with the nuclear separation R, if the sum $U(R)$ of $E(R)$ and the nuclear repulsive energy goes through a minimum. As the appendix shows, that sum does not go through a minimum for this model, but increases monotonically, though of course the sum is less than the corresponding sum for the antisymmetrical case.

Thus again the model is a poor one, and hindsight shows why. The two delta wells provide potentials without any 'range': the electron experiences a negative potential energy only when it is precisely at one or another of the 'nuclei', no matter what the separation R of the 'nuclei' may be. At the same time the model retains, for the nuclear repulsive energy, the long range of the Coulomb potential. In the real case, the potential energy of the electron when it is between the nuclei keeps going down as the nuclei come toward each other (Fig. 5.3). Hence in reality it is increasingly favourable for the electron to take a position between the nuclei, where it will attract both nuclei toward itself and thus toward each other. That increasing tendency is resisted only by the tendency of the electron to reduce its kinetic energy by increasing its de Broglie wavelength.

But even though the model does not provide a stable bond, it illustrates faithfully two important features of a real molecule: (1) the formation, from the atomic states of the two atoms, of a symmetrical and an antisymmetrical state, and (2) the fact that the symmetrical state is the one that might afford a bond. The symmetrical state is often called a *bonding state* of the electron, and the antisymmetrical state is called an *antibonding state*. Squaring the wave functions of Fig. 5.7 for the two states shows (Fig. 5.9) that the bonding state gives a higher probability of finding the electron between the nuclei, in agreement with the picture that bonding is accomplished by the electrostatic attraction of the electron for the nuclei while it is between them.

Indeed that picture is rigorously correct. It has been shown† that the forces that the electrons in a molecule exert on the nuclei are just those that would be exerted according to classical electrostatic theory by a cloud of negative charge distributed according to the probability interpretation of the square of the wave function for the electrons. The equilibrium lengths of the bonds are determined by the point at which the attractive forces, which

† R. P. Feynman, *Phys. Rev.* **56**, 340 (1939).

this cloud of negative charge exerts on the nuclei, are exactly balanced by the electrostatic repulsive forces of the nuclei on one another. From this point of view, the duty of wave mechanics is to determine the density of electronic charge as a function of the space coordinates, for various separations of the nuclei. Then the rest of the calculation can be carried out by using classical electrostatic ideas. But at present the importance of the 'force way' of looking at the problem is conceptual rather than practical. None of the presently available methods for calculating bond energies and interatomic distances uses this procedure: all the methods are 'energy methods'.

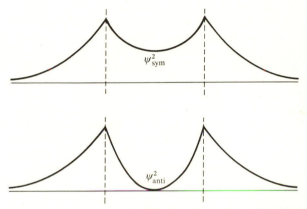

FIG. 5.9. According to the probability interpretation of wave functions, the squares of the two functions shown in Fig. 5.7 measure the relative probability of finding the electron at various places, when it is in a state described by one or the other wave function.

Even though the search in this chapter for a simple one-dimensional model for the hydrogen-molecule ion has yielded none, these trials have clarified the problem. In the light of the preceding discussion, you could easily construct a model that would embody those ingredients, but you might have difficulty finding one that comes usefully close to the facts and at the same time can be easily calculated.

What does this study of the hydrogen-molecule ion lead you to expect when the system acquires another electron and so makes a hydrogen molecule in which the two protons and two electrons form a stable system? The two electrons will both be in the spatially symmetrical state and will have opposite spins. Then, ignoring the electrostatic repulsion between the two electrons for the moment, you can expect that the electronic energy will be twice as great as before at each value of R. Since the nuclear repulsion will be the same as before at each value of R, the minimum total energy will lie at a shorter separation of the nuclei. Thinking in terms of the forces in the system, you can expect to find roughly twice as much negative charge between the nuclei, tending to pull them together. But you cannot easily guess what separation of the nuclei will provide the new force balance, nor what the total energy will be at that separation.

Adding the electrostatic repulsion between the two electrons will make additional corrections in your guess. That interaction will add a repulsive term to the electronic potential energy. Moreover, by making the electrons tend to stay out of each other's way, it will reduce the electronic density between the nuclei and thus reduce the attractive terms in the electronic potential energy.

In experimental fact, the bond length in the hydrogen molecule is 0·74 Å, to be compared with 1·06 Å in the molecule ion. The total energy of the molecule is $-31·7$ eV, to be compared with $-16·3$ eV in the molecule ion. At first it may seem surprising how nearly the energy is doubled by adding the second electron. The addition of a second electron to the helium ion, to form the neutral helium atom, releases less than half the energy that is released by the first electron when it joins the helium nucleus to form the ion.

There is a great quantitative difference between atoms and molecules in this respect. The effect of the repulsion between electrons is more important in an atom because there a single nucleus is attracting several electrons to it. In a molecule the separation of the centres of positive charge gives the several electrons space to move about in a region of low potential energy, without getting in the way of one another.

In one important way, however, both the hydrogen molecule and the molecule ion fail to typify the behaviour of other molecules. Only in these two molecules are the atoms held apart entirely by the electrostatic repulsion between their nuclei. In all other molecules the repulsive force arises primarily from the behaviour of the electrons that are not engaged in bonding. As the atoms come closer to each other, those disengaged electrons are forced into states of higher energy, and so offer a strong repulsion to closer approach. As you saw in Chapter 3, that repulsion grows in strength much more rapidly with decreasing separation than the electrostatic repulsion that keeps the protons apart in the hydrogen molecule. Pursuing in the next two chapters a more penetrating analysis of the electron-pair bond, you will see the origin of that repulsion more clearly.

PROBLEMS

5.1 The energy of the hydrogen atom in its ground state is minus one atomic unit, or $-13·58$ eV. That is the energy of the atom relative to a proton and an electron infinitely separated and at rest. What is the difference in energy between H_2^+ and $H + H^+$? In other words, is the hydrogen-molecule ion stable or unstable relative to one hydrogen atom and one proton infinitely separated, and by how much energy? This quantity is called the *dissociation energy* of the molecule. Compare the experimental value with the value calculated in Discussion 5.1.

5.2   The virial theorem asserts that, in a system of charged mass-points interacting by Coulomb's law, the kinetic energy will be one half the absolute value of the (negative) potential energy when the system is behaving stably. Does the approximation of Discussion 5.1 obey this theorem at the equilibrium separation?

5.3   By looking at the general form of the true wave function for the electron in H_2^+ (for example, Fig. 5.7), you can see that you have been able to get as good an approximation as you have by the crude model of Figs. 5.4 and 5.5 in consequence of making two errors that partially compensate each other. What is the nature of these errors?

5.4   It might occur to you that the delta-well model for H_2^+ contains a conceptual inconsistency (in using the short-range potential of the delta well for the electron–proton interactions, and the long-range Coulomb potential for the proton–proton interactions), which could be removed by representing the proton–proton interaction as a delta spike. Conclude without calculation what internuclear distance, and what total energy, you would obtain as equilibrium values.

APPENDIX

A DELTA-WELL MODEL OF THE HYDROGEN-MOLECULE ION

To find the wave functions for an electron moving in one dimension, in the presence of two delta wells separated by the distance R (Fig. 5.10), write Schrödinger's equation. When written in atomic units,† it is

$$\frac{d^2\psi}{dx^2} + [E - V(x)]\psi = 0. \tag{A5.1}$$

Everywhere outside the wells $V(x) = 0$, and thus for the three ranges of Fig. 5.10 the appropriate solutions are of the form

$$\psi_1 = A e^{kx}, \qquad \psi_3 = B e^{-kx},$$
$$\psi_2 = A_2 e^{kx} + B_2 e^{-kx}, \tag{A5.2}$$

where $k \equiv \sqrt{(-E)}$, and E is negative when the electron is bound to the wells. Matching ψ_1 to ψ_2 at $x = -R/2$, and ψ_2 to ψ_3 at $x = +R/2$, gives

$$A = A_2 + B_2 e^{kR}$$
$$B = B_2 + A_2 e^{kR}. \tag{A5.3}$$

At each well the function will have a discontinuity of slope, obtainable by integrating (A5.1) across the well, and taking the well so narrow that ψ is constant over its width l, and so deep that E is negligible in comparison with V. With the use of these assumptions, (A5.1) becomes

$$d\frac{d\psi}{dx} = V\psi \, dx. \tag{A5.4}$$

Then at the left well

$$\frac{d\psi_2}{dx}\bigg|_{x=-R/2} - \frac{d\psi_1}{dx}\bigg|_{x=-R/2} = \psi(-R/2)Vl, \tag{A5.5}$$

† This method of simplifying the appearance of Schrödinger's equation is described in *Stationary states*, Discussion 9.1, and *The nature of atoms*, Discussion 4.1.

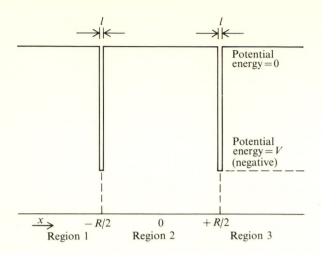

FIG. 5.10. In the delta-well model for the hydrogen-molecule ion, the potential for the electron due to the two protons is simulated by two square potential wells in which $l \to 0$ and $V \to -\infty$ in such a way that $-Vl = \eta$, a positive constant.

and at the right well

$$\frac{\mathrm{d}\psi_3}{\mathrm{d}x}\bigg|_{x=R/2} - \frac{\mathrm{d}\psi_2}{\mathrm{d}x}\bigg|_{x=R/2} = \psi(R/2)Vl. \tag{A5.6}$$

Evaluating (A5.5) and (A5.6), and denoting $Vl \equiv -\eta$ (where η is positive since V is negative), yields

$$A_2 k - B_2 k e^{kR} - Ak = -\eta A,$$
$$B_2 k - A_2 k e^{kR} - Bk = -\eta B. \tag{A5.7}$$

When A and B are eliminated from (A5.7) by using (A5.3),

$$\eta A_2 = (2k - \eta)B_2 e^{kR},$$
$$\eta B_2 = (2k - \eta)A_2 e^{kR}, \tag{A5.8}$$

whose consistency requires

$$e^{kR} = \frac{\pm \eta}{2k - \eta}. \tag{A5.9}$$

When $e^{kR} = +\eta/(2k - \eta)$, (A5.8) gives $A_2 = B_2$, and hence by (A5.3) $A = B$. In this case, therefore, ψ is symmetric about $x = 0$. When $e^{kR} = -\eta/(2k - \eta)$, (A5.8) gives $A_2 = -B_2$, and hence by (A5.3) $A = -B$. In this case ψ is antisymmetric about $x = 0$. In the symmetric case, when $R = 0$, $k = \eta$, or $E = -\eta^2$. As R increases, k decreases, remaining greater than $\eta/2$, and as $R \to \infty$, $k \to \eta/2$, or $E \to -\eta^2/4$.

In the antisymmetric case $k < \eta/2$ for large R, and thus as $R \to \infty$, $k \to \eta/2$ again. As R decreases, so does k, and at the point where k goes through zero and becomes negative, the exponential forms of the solution (A5.2) are no longer acceptable, since they would cause the wave function to increase indefinitely for large positive and negative values of x. Thus for small separations, E will be positive, and (A5.1) will have trigonometric solutions, describing an electron that is not bound to the wells but suffers a change in phase in its wave function as it traverses the wells. The value of R at which this transition occurs can be found by expanding both sides of

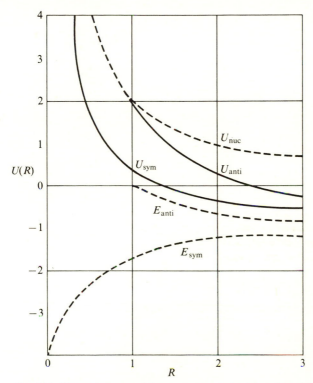

FIG. 5.11. The total energy, and its components, in the delta-well model of the hydrogen-molecule ion, when the electron is in the symmetric and antisymmetric bound states, plotted in atomic units.

(A5.9) for the antisymmetric case in powers of k,

$$1+kR+\dots = 1+\frac{2k}{\eta}+\dots, \tag{A5.10}$$

and finding

$$R \to 2/\eta \quad \text{as} \quad k \to 0.$$

In order to specialize the problem to the hydrogen-molecule ion, take $\eta = 2$, since the energy of the ground state of the hydrogen atom is -1 atomic unit, and $-E \equiv k^2 = \eta^2/4$ for the infinitely separated wells. The value of R obtained from

(A5.9) is

$$R = \frac{1}{k} \log \frac{\pm 1}{k-1}. \tag{A5.11}$$

The plots of Fig. 5.8 can now be made by using this value of R and the value $E(R) = -k^2$. Since the nuclear repulsive energy is $e^2/4\pi\epsilon_0 R$, or $2/R$ in atomic units, $U(R)$ can now be plotted against R (Fig. 5.11) in atomic units, to find that the delta wells fail to provide a true bonding state, for the reasons the text discusses.

6. The Hydrogen Molecule

THE covalent bond between two atoms can be understood quite well by examining the behaviour of a single electron in the presence of two attracting nuclei, as the last chapter pointed out. But the covalent bond is usually formed by two electrons, not one; and the end of the last chapter suggested a way of thinking about how these two electrons behave. It pictured the two electrons in states described by wave functions that show the same spatial dependence, and in which the electrons have opposite spins.

Now this is a rather loose way of thinking about two electrons: it says both more and less than can properly be said about them. For example, by putting each electron separately into a one-electron state, this way of thinking offers no way of estimating the effect of their mutual repulsion, and thus it provides less information than you have a right to ask. On the other hand, by putting both electrons into states with the same spatial dependence, and retaining the exclusion principle, it forces the conclusion that the two electrons must have opposite spins. They usually do, to be sure, but in many important cases, the oxygen molecule, for example, they do not.

These difficulties have arisen out of a mistake that marks this way of thinking about the pair of electrons. We have considered the electrons too much as *two*, and too little as *a pair*. Electrons are indistinguishable particles. One can say how many there are, but one can find no labels that will identify which is which. In consequence, one must examine wave functions that describe states for both electrons together, and one must require that such a wave function should give the same description of a state if the two electrons are interchanged.

It is not difficult to embody this idea in a mathematical programme; it is difficult only to carry through the calculations that the programme prescribes. Schrödinger's equation again provides the necessary mathematical apparatus.† In the present context it is a partial differential equation whose single dependent variable is the desired wave function, a function of the coordinates of both electrons. The part of the equation that contains the potential energy of the electrons includes the instantaneous potential energy of each in the presence of the two nuclei, and also the instantaneous repulsion between them. The solutions that are picked out as physically meaningful are those whose squares retain the same value when the coordinates of the electrons are interchanged.

In order to see what the product of such a programme might be, look for

---

† The procedure is described in *Stationary states*, Chapter 4.

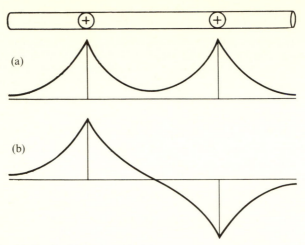

(a)

(b)

FIG. 6.1. For the delta-well model of the hydrogen-molecule ion in Chapter 5, the two one-electron wave functions are spatially symmetrical (a) and anti-symmetrical (b).

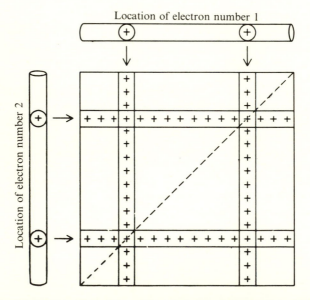

FIG. 6.2. Specifying the positions of the two electrons in the one-dimensional delta-well model of the hydrogen molecule requires a plane instead of a line. The regions marked + show the positions of the wells, and the dashed line shows the points at which the two electrons are coincident.

a moment at the result it would yield when applied to the simple one-dimensional model of the last chapter. Again the two electrons are confined to a line, and two delta wells simulate the attraction of the two nuclei. Representing the positions of each delta well along the line by ⊕, Fig. 6.1 repeats the forms of the two wave functions of lowest energy that were found for one electron in the last chapter. For two electrons the wave function now becomes a function of two variables, the instantaneous positions of the two electrons along the line, and must therefore be plotted as hills and valleys above and below the plane shown in Fig. 6.2. The square of its value at any point in

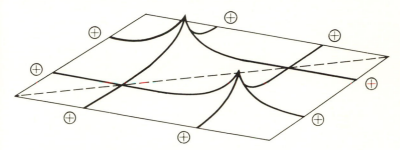

FIG. 6.3. The spatially symmetrical wave function for the two electrons in the delta-well model of the hydrogen molecule has two peaks, for electrons at different wells.

the plane measures the relative probability that the two electrons will be simultaneously at the places represented by the point. The dashed line marks the points that represent the coincidence of the two electrons at one and the same place.

One of the wave functions for this system is shown in Fig. 6.3. The electronic probability is highest near the attracting wells, and some of that probability is pushed away from the places where the electrons are near each other. The wave function is symmetric to a reflection across the dashed line, in obedience to the requirement that the square of its value will not change if the electrons are interchanged.

Another wave function, satisfying all the requirements mentioned so far, is shown in Fig. 6.4. Unlike that shown in Fig. 6.3, it is antisymmetric to reflection across the dashed line: interchanging the electrons changes its sign. But since its square is symmetric, it still makes the same predictions of probability when the two electrons are interchanged, and therefore it is entirely acceptable.

Entering the argument at this point, however, is the behaviour of electrons that is codified in the exclusion principle. Clearly the principle cannot be taken here in the simple form that it has taken in earlier arguments about how two electrons occupy two one-electron wave functions. In this context the exclusion principle must be given its more general form—the form from

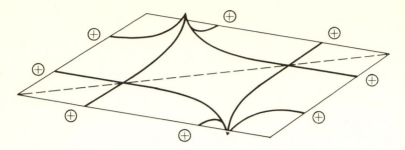

FIG. 6.4. The spatially antisymmetrical wave function for the two electrons in the delta-well model of the hydrogen molecule has two 'peaks' that are of opposite senses.

Discussion 6.1

THE PRINCIPLE OF ANTISYMMETRY

The two-electron wave pictured in Fig. 6.3 is 'symmetric to the interchange of the electrons', because the picture is unaffected by imagining that the electrons have exchanged places. When the pair of electrons is in that state, the exclusion principle asserts that their spins will be opposite. On the other hand, if the two electrons in the wave of Fig. 6.4 exchange places, the wave is turned upside down: every positive number describing the height of its hills and valleys is made negative, and every negative number is made positive. Such a wave is said to be 'antisymmetric to the interchange of the electrons.' And in that case the exclusion principle asserts that their spins will be parallel.

A single rule will cover both cases. Put a number, say the number *one*, to the spin of an electron. Then the spin of another electron receives the same number if it is in the same direction, and the number *minus one* if it is in the opposite direction. Multiplying the two numbers for the spins of the two electrons gives $+1$ if the spins are parallel, -1 if the spins are opposed. Now include, as part of the operation of interchanging the electrons, the operation of multiplying their wave by $+1$ or -1 ($+1$ if their spins are the same, -1 if their spins are opposed). Then the interchange turns the waves of both Figs. 6.3 and 6.4 upside down. In both cases the wave can be called antisymmetric to the interchange of the electrons.

In a fashion such as this, the exclusion principle can be extended to waves for many electrons. The more general form of the principle continues to assert that *electrons are found only in antisymmetrical states*, when their spins are included in the description of their states.

The theory of this property of electrons predicts that no event, of any sort familiar to us, could ever remove electrons from antisymmetric states and put them into symmetric states. But the theory also shows that, if instead the electrons had started life in symmetric states, no event could put them into antisymmetric states.

which the more familiar form can be derived as a consequence in cases where one-electron wave functions provide an adequate approximation.† As Discussion 6.1 describes, the exclusion principle asserts for the case now at hand that the two electrons in the spatially symmetrical wave function (Fig. 6.3) will have opposite spins, and in the spatially antisymmetric wave function (Fig. 6.4) will have spins in the same direction.

From this point of view, therefore, the fact that the electrons in an electron-pair bond usually have opposite spins is due to the fact that in most real cases the state with the spatially symmetrical wave function has the lower energy. But there are cases, such as oxygen, in which the spatially antisymmetrical wave function corresponds with the lower energy. And in any case, the electrons in some bond in a molecule may be excited by outside influences

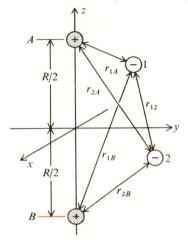

FIG. 6.5. Coordinates for the problem of the electron-pair bond in the hydrogen molecule.

into a state of higher energy that is spatially antisymmetrical, and thus a pair of electrons may exhibit parallel instead of antiparallel spins.‡

In order to make qualitative calculations, an electron-pair bond is often approximated by thinking of it as a suitable combination of the states that the two electrons would have on the two bonded atoms if the atoms were entirely separate. There are two ways of constructing such an approximation. The first method proceeds by taking an atomic wave function on each of the two atoms, placing an electron in each, and then bringing the atoms closer together. The second method makes linear combinations of the two atomic wave functions, each approximating a wave function for the bond such as the last chapter depicted, and then puts in the electrons one after the other.

† The general form of the exclusion principle is discussed in *Stationary states*, Chapter 9.

‡ For spectroscopic reasons, such a state is usually called a *triplet state*.

The rest of this chapter examines the application of both these methods to the electron-pair bond between the two protons in the hydrogen molecule.

In preparation for pursuing the first method, draw and label a picture of the contents of the hydrogen molecule as in Fig. 6.5. The electrons, No. 1 and No. 2, will have states whose wave functions are combinations of the 1s wave functions for two separate hydrogen atoms.

Two such two-electron states can be made out of the two 1s functions of the two atoms. One is symmetric in the spins and antisymmetric in the space-dependent part of the function. Call that space-dependent part ψ_{anti}: interchanging the numbers designating the electrons in ψ_{anti} will reverse its sign.

Discussion 6.2

TRIAL FUNCTIONS FOR THE HYDROGEN MOLECULE

When the atoms are so far apart that their interaction is negligible, and one electron is on each proton, you can write the Schrödinger equations in atomic units,

$$H_{AB}\psi_{AB} \equiv \left[-\nabla_1^2 - \nabla_2^2 - \frac{1}{r_{1A}} - \frac{1}{r_{2B}} \right] \psi_{AB} = 2E_H\psi_{AB},$$

$$H_{BA}\psi_{BA} \equiv \left[-\nabla_1^2 - \nabla_2^2 - \frac{1}{r_{1B}} - \frac{1}{r_{2A}} \right] \psi_{BA} = 2E_H\psi_{BA},$$

depending on which electron is at which proton. Here E_H is one of the energy levels for the hydrogen atom. When they are in their lowest-energy states, both electrons will be in 1s wave functions on their appropriate atoms.

When the atoms interact, you can write, using the coordinates of Fig. 6.5,

$$H\psi \equiv \left[-\nabla_1^2 - \nabla_2^2 - \frac{1}{r_{1A}} - \frac{1}{r_{2B}} - \frac{1}{r_{1B}} - \frac{1}{r_{2A}} + \frac{1}{r_{12}} \right] \psi = E\psi.$$

Recalling the method of solving such equations by separation of variables, you know that a solution of the first of these equations is $A(1) . B(2)$, and a solution of the second is $A(2) . B(1)$. Here $A(1)$, for example, denotes the 1s wave function for hydrogen atom A, written for the coordinates of electron number 1. Since the 1s wave function for hydrogen drops off exponentially with r, the wave function $A(1)$, in the coordinate system of Fig. 6.5, and with distances expressed in atomic units, is

$$A(1) = e^{-r_{1A}},$$

$$r_{1A} = \sqrt{\left\{ x_1^2 + y_1^2 + \left(z_1 - \frac{R}{2} \right)^2 \right\}}.$$

Out of such solutions the trial functions

$$\psi_{sym} = A(1) . B(2) + A(2) . B(1),$$

$$\psi_{anti} = A(1) . B(2) - A(2) . B(1)$$

are constructed with a view to examining how well they approximate true solutions of the third of the Schrödinger equations shown above.

The other two-electron state is antisymmetric in the spins and symmetric (ψ_{sym}) in the space-dependent part. 'Antisymmetric in the spins' means that the spins are opposite: interchanging the numbers designating the electrons in the wave function reverses the spins of both. As Discussion 6.2 shows, the desired wave functions might be written:

$$\psi_{sym} = A(1) \,.\, B(2) + A(2) \,.\, B(1),$$
$$\psi_{anti} = A(1) \,.\, B(2) - A(2) \,.\, B(1),$$

(6.1)

where $A(1)$, for example, means the wave function for hydrogen atom A, written for the coordinates of electron No. 1.

Discussion 6.3

DISTRIBUTION OF ELECTRONS

The squares of the wave functions given by the expressions (6.1) are

$$\psi^2 = A^2(1) \,.\, B^2(2) + A^2(2) \,.\, B^2(1) \pm 2A(1) \,.\, B(2) \,.\, A(2) \,.\, B(1),$$

where $+$ applies to ψ_{sym} and $-$ applies to ψ_{anti}. In order to examine the prediction that this makes along the line connecting the two protons, substitute the values of the atomic wave functions shown in Discussion 6.2, and let $x_1 = y_1 = x_2 = y_2 = 0$. Then

$$\psi^2_{line} = \exp -2\,[|z_1 - R/2| + |z_2 + R/2|\,] + \exp -2\,[\,|z_2 - R/2| + |z_1 + R/2|\,] \pm$$
$$\pm 2 \exp - [|z_1 - R/2| + |z_2 - R/2| + |z_1 + R/2| + |z_2 + R/2|\,].$$

At the middle of the line between the two protons $z_1 = z_2 = 0$. Substituting these values of the z's in the preceding expression shows that the probability that the two electrons are both midway between the protons, in their strongest bonding positions, is proportional:

for ψ_{sym} to $4e^{-2R}$,

for ψ_{anti} to 0.

Suppose for the moment that these functions do approximate two possible electronic wave functions for the hydrogen molecule. Then some of the physical differences between them can be examined by looking at their squares, which will measure the probability that electron No. 1 is in the region around x_1, y_1, z_1, and electron No. 2 is in the region around x_2, y_2, z_2. For example, as Discussion 6.3 shows, the probability that the two electrons are both midway between the protons, in their strongest bonding positions, is finite when they are in the state described by ψ_{sym} and increases with decreasing separation of the protons. On the other hand the wave function ψ_{anti} vanishes for that position of the electrons. When this kind of job is done throughout the space around the protons, the contours of equal electron density turn out to look like Fig. 6.6.

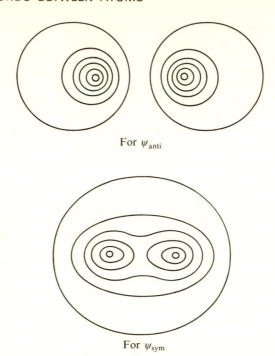

For ψ_{anti}

For ψ_{sym}

FIG. 6.6. Contours of equal electron density, in a plane containing the two nuclei,
for the spatially antisymmetric and symmetric wave functions of (6.1).

Thus it seems possible, from Fig. 6.6, that ψ_{sym} will be a state that bonds
the two protons by piling up negative charge between them. Looking back
at the expression for probability density in Discussion 6.3, you see why this
piling up takes place. The first two terms in that expression are merely the
terms coming from the two separate atoms. The last term appears because
the electrons can exchange places: it is an *exchange* term. Clearly this term
has its largest absolute value where the 1s wave functions for the two atoms
overlap. In the case of ψ_{sym} this term brings more electron density into that
region than the overlapping of the atoms would provide by way of the first
two terms. In the case of ψ_{anti} the overlap tends to push electron density away
from the overlapping region, again more than the mutual repulsion of the
electrons would accomplish by itself.

Notice that this effect is a result of a very general feature of wave mechanics.
A state made up by adding together two component states will not usually
have properties that are simply the sums of the corresponding properties of
those two component states. That is because observable properties of a state
all depend on the *square* of the wave function, in one guise or another. The
expression in Discussion 6.3 for the probability density shows the result of

this clearly in its last term, for the first two terms are simply the squares of the wave functions for the component states.

Now of course the validity of these trial functions still swims in a sea of physical intuition. The functions ψ_{sym} and ψ_{anti} are certainly not exact solutions of Schrödinger's equation for the hydrogen molecule, and nothing up to this point has shown whether they are good or bad approximations. The only way to find out is to calculate some observable properties with the aid of these wave functions and check them against experimental results.

The most important single property to calculate is the energy as a function of the separation of the protons—the $E(R)$ discussed in the last chapter. Then you can see whether the sum of $E(R)$ and the repulsive energy of the two protons goes through a minimum at some value of R. Using the reasoning of the last chapter, you would check that value R_0 against the known inter-atomic distance in the hydrogen molecule, and the corresponding energy U_0 against the known binding energy of the molecule.

It turns out that the check, carried out in the appendix to this chapter, gives a very satisfying answer. Such a check does not rigorously show whether the wave functions themselves are good approximations, but only whether they are capable of yielding good approximations to the energy. Some additional faith in the form of the wave functions, however, comes from the physically sensible reasoning used in constructing them.

It is convenient to have a word for the space-dependent part of a wave function for one electron, to distinguish it from the whole wave function which includes reference to the spin. *Orbital* is the customary word. Such a function as the 1s wave function, obtained by solving Schrödinger's equation for an atom, is called an *atomic orbital*. Such functions as the wave functions used in the last chapter for the hydrogen-molecule ion are called *molecular orbitals*. The foregoing method of approximation in a many-electron problem is therefore often called the *atomic orbital method*.

Look now at the other way of picturing the hydrogen molecule—a *molecular orbital method*, in which the orbitals for the hydrogen-molecule ion are filled with two electrons in succession. As the last chapter remarked, Schrödinger's equation can be solved for an electron in the presence of two protons separated by the distance R, but the solutions cannot be expressed in closed form in terms of familiar functions. Of the two solutions corresponding to the lowest energies in the interesting region of R, one is spatially symmetric, the other antisymmetric, with respect to the perpendicular plane bisecting the line between the two protons. Fig. 6.7 shows roughly the character of the wave functions along the line of the protons.

Now consider the ways in which two electrons can occupy these molecular orbitals. To follow convention, call the spatially symmetric orbital σ_g (g = *gerade* = even) and the spatially antisymmetric orbital σ_u (u = *ungerade* = odd). The two electrons will obey the exclusion principle if they are in any of the wave functions shown in Table 6.1.

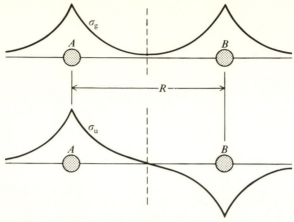

FIG. 6.7. The general form of cross-sections of the spatially symmetric (*gerade*) and spatially antisymmetric (*ungerade*) wave functions for the hydrogen molecule.

The question now arises, why does the molecular orbital method afford four possibilities, three with spins paired, whereas the atomic orbital method seemed to yield only two possibilities, one with spins paired? The answer comes from looking at a way of approximating σ_g and σ_u in terms of 'A' and 'B': the 1s wave functions on the two atoms, which you used before. This way of approximating molecular orbitals is often called the *LCAO approximation*: the linear combination of atomic orbitals. Fig. 6.8 shows cross-sections of A and B. Clearly $A + B$ looks like σ_g (Fig. 6.7) and $A - B$ looks like σ_u. By using these approximations, the four functions of Table 6.1 can be rewritten into the forms shown in Table 6.2. When the products in Table 6.2 are expanded, and the results are compared with (6.1), the four functions take the forms shown in Table 6.3.

These forms now call attention to two combinations of the atomic orbitals that were neglected in the earlier pursuit of the atomic orbital method: the combinations $A(1) . A(2)$ and $B(1) . B(2)$. Clearly the states that these combinations represent are those in which both electrons with spins paired, are on one or the other proton: the 'ionic states' H^-H^+ and H^+H^- (Fig. 6.9). It is altogether probable that an approximation to the true wave function

TABLE 6.1

1	$\sigma_g(1) . \sigma_g(2)$	Spins opposite
2	$\sigma_u(1) . \sigma_u(2)$	Spins opposite
3	$\sigma_g(1) . \sigma_u(2) + \sigma_u(1) . \sigma_g(2)$	Spins opposite
4	$\sigma_g(1) . \sigma_u(2) - \sigma_u(1) . \sigma_g(2)$	Spins parallel

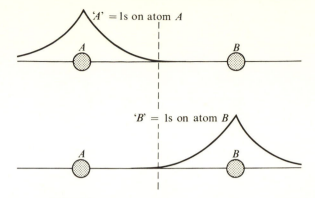

‘A’ = 1s on atom A

‘B’ = 1s on atom B

Fig. 6.8. Cross-sections of the atomic 1s wave functions on two hydrogen atoms, whose sum and difference approximate the two molecular wave functions of Fig. 6.7.

for the hydrogen molecule would be better if it included a little of these combinations along with ψ_{sym}. They cannot be used with ψ_{anti} because in the ionic combinations the spins are antiparallel, and in ψ_{anti} the spins are parallel.

The way to effect this improvement in the approximation is to add to ψ_{sym} proportions C_A of $A(1) \cdot A(2)$ and C_B of $B(1) \cdot B(2)$. For the hydrogen

TABLE 6.2

1	$[A(1)+B(1)] \cdot [A(2)+B(2)]$
2	$[A(1)-B(1)] \cdot [A(2)-B(2)]$
3	$[A(1)+B(1)] \cdot [A(2)-B(2)] + [A(1)-B(1)] \cdot [A(2)+B(2)]$
4	$[A(1)+B(1)] \cdot [A(2)-B(2)] - [A(1)-B(1)] \cdot [A(2)+B(2)]$

molecule, whose two atoms are identical, you can take $C_A = C_B \equiv C$. When the bonded atoms differ, C_A may not equal C_B, and their inequality will betoken a mixture of ionic and covalent bonding. In order to determine the best value of C, you can use the fact that the molecule will surely choose that value that gives it the lowest energy.†

TABLE 6.3

1	$A(1) \cdot A(2) + B(1) \cdot B(2) + \psi_{sym}$
2	$A(1) \cdot A(2) + B(1) \cdot B(2) - \psi_{sym}$
3	$2[A(1) \cdot A(2) - B(1) \cdot B(2)]$
4	$-2\psi_{anti}$

† This idea can be embodied in a calculation by using the *variational method* described in *Stationary states*, Chapter 7.

$A(1) \cdot B(2)$

$A(2) \cdot B(1)$

$A(1) \cdot A(2)$

$B(1) \cdot B(2)$

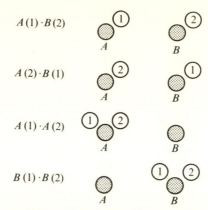

Fig. 6.9. Four combinations of atomic states that can contribute to the bonding of two atoms by a pair of electrons. The upper two are those used in the approximations of (6.1); the lower two are 'ionic' or 'polar' states.

Alternatively, a similar procedure could be followed with the first three molecular orbitals in Table 6.1. Either procedure will lead finally to two molecular states, constructed either from the two atomic orbitals A and B or the two molecular orbitals σ_g and σ_u. In one of these states, a bonding state, the spins of the electrons will be opposed, and the energy will pass through a minimum as R varies. In the other state, an antibonding state, the spins will be parallel, and the state will repel the protons at all values of R. This sort of analysis has been applied to other atoms as well as hydrogen, and its results can be summarized in a few useful generalizations.

In the first place, when molecular orbitals are made by taking *linear combinations of atomic orbitals*, the number of finally independent molecular orbitals is always the same as the number of atomic orbitals employed. In the example of this chapter, the number is two. Usually half the molecular orbitals are bonding orbitals and half are antibonding. Since each orbital will hold only two electrons, the number of electrons involved in bonding will not exceed the number of atomic orbitals that have been invoked. When these numbers are equal, the molecule shows *saturated valency* on the part of all its atoms. When there are fewer electrons available for bonding than the number of atomic orbitals involved in the bonding, the bonds are called *electron-deficient bonds*.

Usually the bonding orbitals that lie lowest in the energy scale are orbitals for states in which the spins are opposed. Most of the molecules in nature are bonded by pairs of electrons with opposed spins; but there are exceptions, of which molecular oxygen is the most familiar. In oxygen two of the four bonding electrons have parallel spins because there is an *orbital degeneracy*; two bonding orbitals have the same energy. Of the resulting bonding states, one is a state with spins opposed, the other with spins parallel.

Most importantly, however, the analysis reemphasizes the picture of bonding as an accumulation of negative charge between the positive nuclei—the picture already presented in the last chapter. You can see two opposing tendencies at work. The electrons tend to push each other away. But this is outweighed by the fact that the potential energy of all of them is lowest when they are between the nuclei. They would all rush there, and everything would form bonds with everything else, were it not for the behaviour described by the exclusion principle. In accordance with that principle they find states that are antisymmetric to their interchange. As in atoms, so in molecules, that law of antisymmetry limits the occupancy of each orbital. Only some of the states will give electron densities favourable for bonding.

The bonding states, having energy minima with respect to variations of the nuclear arrangement, are those that permit the electronic charge to accumulate between the nuclei. When those bonding states are viewed as constructed out of atomic orbitals, the accumulation of charge is greatest where the atomic orbitals would overlap the most. And the accumulation is greater than that overlap alone would provide, in consequence of an exchange effect that augments the simple sum.

APPENDIX

BINDING ENERGY OF HYDROGEN BY THE METHOD OF ATOMIC ORBITALS

The expectation value of the true energy† will be $E(R) = \int \psi H \psi \, d\tau$, where H is the Hamiltonian operator used in Schrödinger's equation for the true case (Discussion 6.2) and ψ is the true wave function, properly normalized. The same method can be used here to calculate approximate energies, by employing the true Hamiltonian and the approximate wave functions ψ_{sym} and ψ_{anti} (6.1), taking care of normalization by dividing by $\int \psi^2 \, d\tau$:

$$E(R) = \frac{\int \psi H \psi \, d\tau}{\int \psi^2 \, d\tau}. \tag{A6.1}$$

Look first at the normalization integral in the denominator: it is the integral, over all the coordinates, of the expression in Discussion 6.3. Its first two terms are

$$\int A^2(1) \, d\tau_1 \cdot \int B^2(2) \, d\tau_2 + \int A^2(2) \, d\tau_2 \cdot \int B^2(1) \, d\tau_1.$$

If $A(1)$ etc. are chosen as the normalized solutions to the hydrogen-atom problem, each integral equals unity by the definition of normalization. The last term breaks into the product

$$\pm 2 \int A(1) \cdot B(1) \, d\tau_1 \cdot \int A(2) \cdot B(2) \, d\tau_2.$$

Since both the integrals in this product have the same mathematical form, the product is a square, and therefore essentially positive. Often denoted by S, it has the value

$$S = e^{-2R}(1 + R + \tfrac{1}{3}R^2)^2. \tag{A6.2}$$

† The calculation of wave-mechanical expectation values is described in *Stationary states*.

Thus the denominator is

$$\int \psi^2 \, d\tau = 2(1 \pm S). \tag{A6.3}$$

The integral in the numerator can be broken up also. From the first two equations of Discussion 6.2,

$$H = H_{AB} - \frac{1}{r_{1B}} - \frac{1}{r_{2A}} + \frac{1}{r_{12}} = H_{BA} - \frac{1}{r_{1A}} - \frac{1}{r_{2B}} + \frac{1}{r_{12}}. \tag{A6.4}$$

Since each of the two parts of the approximate solutions is a solution to one of those equations,

$$H_{AB}[A(1) \cdot B(2)] = 2E_H[A(1) \cdot B(2)],$$
$$H_{BA}[A(2) \cdot B(1)] = 2E_H[A(2) \cdot B(1)]. \tag{A6.5}$$

By the use of (A6.4) and (A6.5) the integrand in the numerator of (A6.1) becomes

$$\psi H \psi = [A(1) \cdot B(2) \pm A(2) \cdot B(1)] \cdot \left\{ 2E_H[A(1) \cdot B(2) \pm A(2) \cdot B(1)] + \right.$$
$$\left. + \left(\frac{1}{r_{12}} - \frac{1}{r_{1B}} - \frac{1}{r_{2A}} \right) A(1) \cdot B(2) \pm \left(\frac{1}{r_{12}} - \frac{1}{r_{1A}} - \frac{1}{r_{2B}} \right) A(2) \cdot B(1) \right\}$$
$$= 4E_H(1 \pm s) + \left(\frac{1}{r_{12}} - \frac{1}{r_{1B}} - \frac{1}{r_{2A}} \right) A^2(1) \cdot B^2(2) +$$
$$+ \left(\frac{1}{r_{12}} - \frac{1}{r_{1A}} - \frac{1}{r_{2B}} \right) A^2(2) \cdot B^2(1) \pm$$
$$\pm \left[\left(\frac{1}{r_{12}} - \frac{1}{r_{1B}} - \frac{1}{r_{2A}} \right) + \left(\frac{1}{r_{12}} - \frac{1}{r_{2A}} - \frac{1}{r_{1B}} \right) \right] \times$$
$$\times A(1) \cdot B(2) \cdot A(2) \cdot B(1). \tag{A6.6}$$

The terms in the integral of the expression (A6.6) can again be identified as equivalent in pairs because they have the same mathematical form: they merely

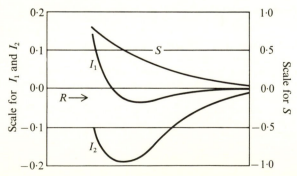

FIG. 6.10. Integrals, as functions of internuclear separation, for an approximation to the electronic part of the binding energy of the hydrogen molecule.

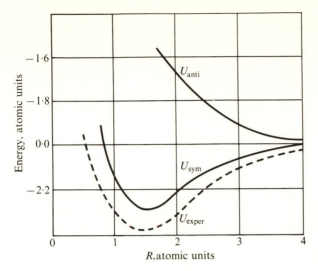

FIG. 6.11. Total energy $(E(R) + e^2/4\pi\epsilon_0 R)$ of the hydrogen molecule, calculated by the method of approximation embodied in (6.1).

have the labels 1 and 2 interchanged on their variables of integration. The integral can therefore be written in the form

$$\int \psi H \psi \, d\tau = 4E_H(1 \pm S) + 2(I_1 \pm I_2), \tag{A6.7}$$

where

$$I_1 = \int \left(\frac{1}{r_{12}} - \frac{1}{r_{1A}} - \frac{1}{r_{2B}} \right) A^2(2) \cdot B^2(1) \, d\tau, \tag{A6.8}$$

and

$$I_2 = \int \left(\frac{1}{r_{12}} - \frac{1}{r_{1A}} - \frac{1}{r_{2B}} \right) A(1) \cdot B(1) \cdot A(2) \cdot B(2) \, d\tau. \tag{A6.9}$$

Hence finally

$$E(R) = 2E_H + \frac{I_1 \pm I_2}{1 \pm S}, \tag{A6.10}$$

where $+$ applies to the state ψ_{sym} and $-$ applies to the state ψ_{anti}.

The integral I_1 is easily evaluated, but the integral I_2 is not. Instead of going into mathematical detail, accept the results shown graphically in Fig. 6.10. By adding to them the repulsive energy $e^2/4\pi\epsilon_0 R$ of the two protons, Fig. 6.11 can be drawn for the energy $U(R)$ of the molecule. The values of R_0 and U_{min} obtained for the molecule in the state ψ_{sym} are 0·8 Å, and $-3·16$ eV, to be compared with the experimental values of 0·74 Å and $-4·75$ eV.

In comparing the value of $U_{\text{min}} = -4·75$ eV with the value of $U_0 = -31·7$ eV cited at the end of the last chapter, notice that U_0 refers to a zero of energy in which the molecule is entirely dispersed into protons and electrons that are all far from one another, whereas U_{min} refers to a zero of energy in which two hydrogen atoms are separated. Hence the difference corresponds to twice the ionization potential of hydrogen: $2 \times 13·5$ eV . U_{min} is called the *dissociation energy* of the molecule.

Figs. 6.10 and 6.11 show that the major contribution to the difference between the energies of the symmetric and antisymmetric states of the molecule, in the interesting region of R, has come from the integral I_2. (A6.9) shows that this integral contains the combination of the component one-electron wave functions that was found responsible for piling up or pushing away the electron density between the protons (Discussion 6.3). This integral is called the *exchange integral*. The fact that it is negative makes the state ψ_{sym}, with the spins of the two electrons antiparallel or 'paired', the state with the lower energy. Since that state shows a minimum as R varies, it is able to provide a bond between the protons: it is a *bonding state* of the molecule. The other state, which is repulsive for all values of R, and in which the two spins are parallel, is an *antibonding state*.

7. The Spatial Properties of Bonds

THE discussion of the last chapter has constructed a picture of covalent bonding that can be codified for many purposes into the following rules. A covalent bond forms when (1) the atomic orbitals of two atoms overlap, (2) an electron in each atom can exchange with an electron in its partner atom without violating the exclusion principle, and (3) the resulting exchange leads to an increased electronic density between the atoms. And that last

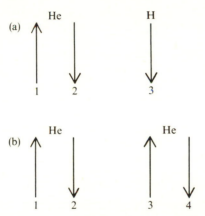

FIG. 7.1. A helium atom does not form a covalent bond with a hydrogen atom (a), or with another helium atom (b).

condition is usually fulfilled only when the two exchanging electrons have opposite spins.

Examine a schematic way of studying the operation of these rules in Fig. 7.1, where the electrons and their spins, up and down, are numbered and shown by arrows associated with symbols for the atoms whose bonding is in question. For example, in the attempt of the helium atom, with two 1s electrons, to form a bond with the hydrogen atom with one 1s electron (Fig. 7.1(a)), two alternative exchanges among the three electrons can be visualized. If No. 1 exchanges with No. 3, the helium atom will have No. 2 and No. 3 in the same atomic orbital, which the exclusion principle forbids because their spins are the same. On the other hand, if No. 2 exchanges with No. 3, the exchange will be antibonding because the exchanging spins are the same. Hence no HeH molecule is to be expected, and in fact that species has not been found in nature. Similarly, of the possible exchanges between the two helium atoms (Fig. 7.1(b)), the exchanges of No. 1 and No. 4, and of No. 2 and No. 3, would violate the exclusion principle, and the exchanges of No. 1 and No. 3, and of No. 2 and No. 4, would be antibonding.

Notice as you go that the only behaviour of these electrons not prohibited by the exclusion principle finds them in antibonding orbitals. The last chapter showed (Fig. 6.6) that in such an orbital electron density is pushed away from the space between the nuclei, and also (Fig. 6.11) that the electronic energy increases rapidly as the distance between the nuclei shortens. Here is the principal origin of the repulsive force between atoms. When the atoms approach each other they bounce away, as if they were balls that are only slightly compressible, because their electrons are forced into antibonding orbitals.

In order to extend the reasoning, begun with hydrogen and helium, to atoms that contain more than two electrons, recall the ways in which electrons occupy the one-electron states that an atom presents. In building up the periodic table of the elements by the *aufbauprinzip*, each successive atom receives one more electron, whose negative charge is compensated by an increased positive charge on the nucleus. That electron enters the state of lowest energy not already fully occupied. According to the exclusion principle each state is fully occupied when it has been adopted by two electrons, and then those electrons necessarily have opposed spins. The relative energies of the one-electron states can be qualitatively shown in a diagram like Fig. 7.2, where boxes symbolize the states, and their relative energies are suggested by the height at which the boxes appear.

For the first ten elements in the periodic table the occupancies of these atomic states are shown in Fig. 7.3. Each occupying electron is represented by an arrow, and the fact that the spins of two electrons in the same one-electron state are opposed is symbolized by directing the arrows oppositely. In general only the electrons in the occupied states of highest energy will participate in bonding; electrons in states of lower energy are too tightly bound within their parent atom to visit another. When atoms are pulled toward one another by bonding forces of any sort, the electrons that completely occupy the states of lower energy in them are forced into antibonding orbitals and so hold the atoms apart, giving to each atom an effective size and to each bond an effective length.

Such diagrams as those in Fig. 7.3 can now be used to symbolize how the proposed rules for covalent bonding operate with the higher-energy electrons in these atoms. The oxygen atom has two 1s electrons, two 2s electrons, and four 2p electrons, of which the last six are shown in Fig. 7.4(a). In forming the water molecule, H_2O, each hydrogen atom exchanges its electron with one of the 2p electrons in the oxygen atom. In the ammonia molecule, NH_3 (Fig. 7.4(b)), three hydrogen atoms exchange an electron in a similar way with a nitrogen atom. Fig. 7.4(c) diagrams the diatomic fluorine molecule according to the present scheme.

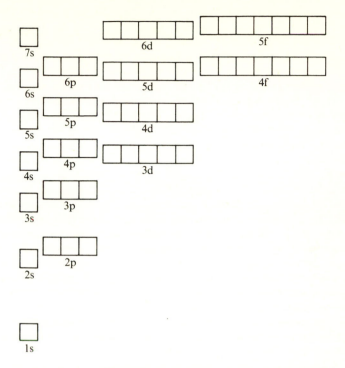

Fig. 7.2. Boxes, each of which can accommodate at most two electrons of opposite spin, symbolize qualitatively the energy sequence of the one-electron states in a many-electron atom.

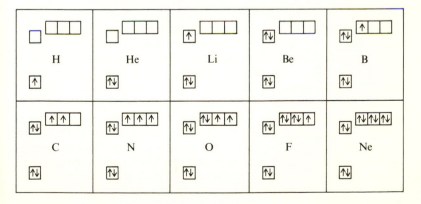

Fig. 7.3. Electron configurations in the ground states of atoms of the first ten elements in the periodic table, shown by the method of Fig. 7.2.

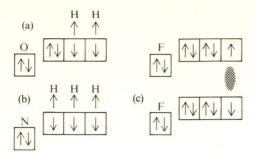

FIG. 7.4. The exchanges which make possible the bonds in (a) H_2O, (b) NH_3, and (c) F_2.

The single electron in a hydrogen atom is in a state that has spherical symmetry about the proton. But the electrons in the oxygen atom and the nitrogen atom that participate in the bonding formalized in Fig. 7.4 are in p states, which are not spherically symmetrical. In any one such atom the different p states give electronic densities whose maxima project in different directions, as Fig. 7.5 shows. Hence if covalent bonding is strongest when the wave functions of the participating atoms can overlap the most, as the last chapter suggested, one would expect to find that the angles between the bonds to the several hydrogen atoms in water and ammonia would correspond with the angles between the maxima in Fig. 7.5, as shown in Fig. 7.6.

The experimentally determined angles are actually not 90°, but 105° in water and 109° in ammonia. The differences are probably due to the fact that the bonds are not purely covalent but are partly ionic. The last chapter showed that the states H^+H^- and H^-H^+ might contribute appreciably to the completed atomic-orbital picture of the hydrogen molecule. When the two bonded atoms are not of the same species, the two ionic states will usually not contribute equally. Which one will predominate depends on atomic details of participating atoms summarized as their *relative electronegativity*. In the cases of water and ammonia, there are appreciable contributions from ionic states of the type H^+O^-H and HO^-H^+, shown in Fig. 7.7. Hence the hydrogen atoms tend to repel one another, and the configuration of lowest energy shows a larger bond angle than the p bond angle.

This idea can be checked by comparing the measured bond angles and dipole moments of water (H_2O) and hydrogen sulphide (H_2S), and of ammonia (NH_3) and phosphine (PH_3), tabulated in Fig. 7.8. Here sulphur and phosphorus are also bonding by electrons that are in atomic p orbitals. But from other evidence sulphur and phosphorus are known to be less electronegative than oxygen and nitrogen.

Look now at the character of the bonds between two atoms that are exchanging more than one pair of electrons. The nitrogen molecule, for

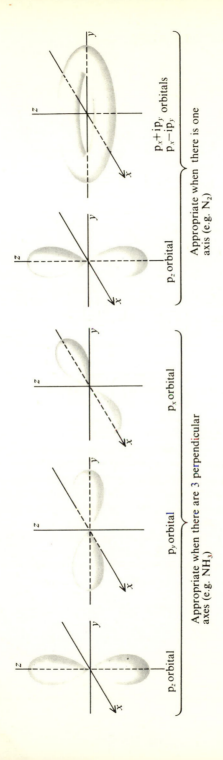

Fig. 7.5. The angular dependence of the squares of the p orbitals. These multiply the squares of the radial dependences to yield the squares of the orbitals.

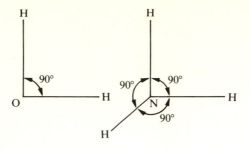

FIG. 7.6. The bond angles in H_2O and NH_3 that Fig. 7.5 would suggest.

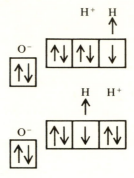

FIG. 7.7. The ionic contributions to the bonding in H_2O.

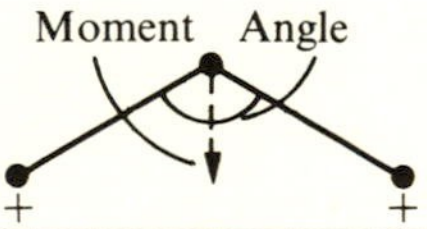

	Bond angle	Dipole moment $(C\ m \times 10^{30})$
H_2O	105°	6·13
H_2S	92°	3·10
NH_3	109°	4·86
PH_3	93°	1·83

FIG. 7.8. Evidence that the departure of actual bond angles from those which Fig. 7.5 would suggest is caused by ionic contributions to the bonding.

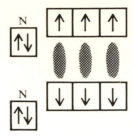

FIG. 7.9. The exchanges in the triply bonded nitrogen molecule.

example, consists of two nitrogen atoms, and the exchanges could be schematized as in Fig. 7.9. As Fig. 7.5 shows, the three 2p atomic orbitals of the two atoms cannot all overlap to their maximum. The line between the two atoms establishes a z axis; one can expect that the p_z orbitals will be directed along that line and will exhibit maximum overlap, and the p_x and p_y orbitals, directed at right angles to z, will overlap less. Bonds formed by the overlapping of atomic s orbitals, and of atomic p orbitals directed along the line of the bond, are often called σ *bonds*; and bonds formed by the overlapping of p orbitals that are directed at right angles to the bond are called π *bonds*.

At first glance one would expect that the *triple bond* in nitrogen would be stronger than a single bond, but not three times as strong. Actually the multiplicity of the bond tends to strengthen each of its components somewhat. The increased number of components to the bond pulls the atoms closer together; and by thus increasing the overlap in each component, it increases the strength of each. Table 7.1 shows how this effect is reflected in the measured properties of the diatomic molecules formed by the atoms in the first period of the periodic table.

In showing boron and carbon as having valencies of one and two, and beryllium as zero-valent like the rare gases, Table 7.1 accurately reflects their behaviour in these diatomic molecules but in almost no other chemical respect. The normal valencies of beryllium, boron, and carbon are two, three, and four respectively, as their positions in the periodic table suggest. The reason for their higher valency lies in the relatively low energy required

TABLE 7.1 *Properties of diatomic molecules*

	Li—Li	B—B	C=C	N≡N	O=O	F—F
Interatomic distance (angstroms)	2·67		1·31	1·09	1·21	1·45
Dissociation energy (electron volts per molecule)	1·13	3·00	3·61	9·78	5·09	3·13

to excite one of their 2s electrons to a 2p state. If the energy gained by forming additional bonds more than compensates for the excitation energy, the atom will form those bonds. Thus the fact that the two outermost electrons in beryllium completely fill the 2s orbital does not exclude bonding, as does the filling of the 1s state in helium. The energy required to excite one electron from the 2s to the 2p orbital in beryllium is only 2·7 eV, whereas the energy required to excite one of the 1s electrons of helium to the 2s orbital is 10 eV. For most bonding purposes, therefore, the states of beryllium, boron, and carbon can be imagined to be the excited states schematized in Fig. 7.10.

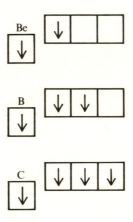

FIG. 7.10. Readily excited states of the beryllium, boron, and carbon atoms account for their valencies.

An interesting problem now arises in examining the bonds formed by carbon. According to the scheme of the excited state shown in Fig. 7.10, carbon should form single bonds of two sorts, one bond using its 2s orbital and three using its 2p orbitals. In fact, however, methane (CH_4) and other such molecules have properties that can be explained only by supposing that all four hydrogens are bonded in the same way, with the same strength, at tetrahedral angles. This fact can best be explained by the hypothesis that *hybrid orbitals* are formed from combinations of the s and p orbitals, as described in Discussion 7.1.

The angular dependence of any one of these orbitals is shown in cross-section in Fig. 7.11; they differ only in the direction of maximum density. The four directions are those from the centre toward the four corners of a regular tetrahedron, and each is cylindrically symmetrical about its direction. The bonds formed by these orbitals are called sp^3 *hybrids*.

Carbon can also form double bonds, and here a different hybridization appears. Only two of the p orbitals are combined with the s orbital, in a way

Discussion 7.1

sp³ HYBRIDIZATION

In the formation of hybrid orbitals it is assumed that the proximity of other atoms so modifies the character of the one 2s and the three 2p orbitals of an atom that their energies are sufficiently close to make them degenerate (see *Stationary States*, Chapter 6). Then any linear combination of them is also a possible orbital. In particular, you can make the combinations

$$\psi_1 = \tfrac{1}{2}(s + p_x + p_y + p_z),$$
$$\psi_2 = \tfrac{1}{2}(s - p_x - p_y + p_z),$$
$$\psi_3 = \tfrac{1}{2}(s - p_x + p_y - p_z),$$
$$\psi_4 = \tfrac{1}{2}(s + p_x - p_y - p_z).$$

The constituent atomic orbitals are orthogonal; and if they are also normalized, these hybrid orbitals can be seen to be normal and orthogonal by forming their squares and products. Since the s function is spherically symmetrical, and since the angular dependence of p_x, p_y, and p_z is proportional to x/r, y/r, and z/r, respectively, the four sp³ hybrids can be seen to have their maxima directed respectively toward the four corners of a tetrahedron centred at the origin of coordinates.

that produces three orbitals whose maximum densities are directed at 120° to one another in the (x, y) plane. Fig. 7.12 shows in cross-section the angular dependence of their electron density. The double bond then consists of one σ bond, formed by one of these sp² *orbitals* and a π bond formed by the remaining p_z orbital, whose maximum density is perpendicular to the plane of the sp² bonds.

Finally, carbon can form a triple bond. Here two orbitals, in opposite directions along the z axis, are formed by hybridizing the s and p_z orbitals. One of the hybrid orbitals forms the σ bond and the p_x and p_y orbitals form the two π bonds, in much the same way that the three p orbitals of nitrogen

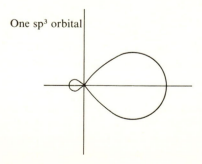

One sp³ orbital

FIG. 7.11. Cross-section of the angular factor in one of the four sp³ hybrid orbitals directed toward the corners of a tetrahedron.

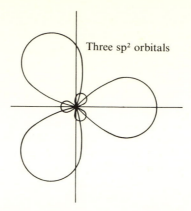

FIG. 7.12. Cross-section of the squares of the three sp² hybrid orbitals, directed at 120° to one another in the plane of the paper.

form the triple bond in the nitrogen molecule. The remaining sp *orbital* forms a σ bond to another atom, to saturate the valency of carbon.

Fig. 7.13 shows examples of the three bonding schemes in ethane (H_3C—CH_3), ethylene (H_2C=CH_2), and acetylene (HC≡CH), in schematic form. Notice an interesting result of the double bond in ethylene; the hydrogen atoms are constrained to lie in the same plane, perpendicular to

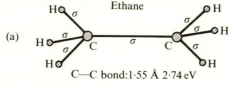

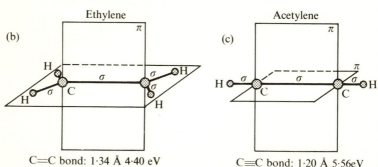

FIG. 7.13. The σ and π bonds in (a) ethane (H_3C—CH_3), (b) ethylene (H_2C=CH_2), and (c) acetylene (HC≡CH) molecules. The planes marked π are the planes determined by the axes of the p orbitals in the atoms that overlap to form a bond.

the plane of the π bond. Molecular spectroscopy shows that in fact ethylene has a high torsional stiffness. In ethane the only interference with the free rotation of one CH_3 group relative to the other about their common axis is caused by the slight repulsive forces between the hydrogen atoms.

In these ways the pictures used by chemists for nearly a century, in which covalent bonds are represented by sticks projecting from holes in the bonded atoms, are remarkably well justified. Like sticks, the bonds have determinable lengths. Like sticks, they project from the atoms at determinable angles. A single bond permits groups of atoms to rotate fairly freely about it, much as a stick would permit them. And atoms that are connected by several bonds are restrained from rotating about them, much as sticks would restrain them.

PROBLEMS

7.1 From the most recent calculations, it appears probable that the helium hydride ion $(HeH)^+$ is a stable species with dissociation energy between 1·75 and 2·05 eV. Use the method of the discussion at the beginning of this chapter to show why this ion might be a stable species whereas the neutral HeH molecule would not.

7.2 (a) Picture the bonding in the BeO molecule by a diagram like Fig. 7.2(c) and Fig. 7.7, on the assumption that the bond is purely covalent.
(b) Using the argument that atoms in molecules attempt to adopt the electronic configurations of the rare gases, do you expect to find an important ionic ingredient in the BeO bond, and if so, in which direction will the dipole moment point?

7.3 (a) Picture the bonding in the carbon dioxide molecule in the manner of Problem 7.2(a).
(b) Since the CO_2 molecule is in fact linear, picture the bonding in the manner of Fig. 7.11, on the assumption that the carbon atom bonds each oxygen atom by a σ bond that is an sp_z hybrid and by a π bond that is a p_x orbital for one oxygen atom and a p_y orbital for the other.

7.4 From the considerations in Problems 7.2 and 7.3, give a reason why at ordinary temperatures carbon dioxide is a gas and beryllium oxide is a solid.

8. Mesomerism and Electron-deficient Bonds

THE discussions of ionic bonding forces in Chapter 3 and of dispersion forces in Chapter 4 pointed out that those forces can form bonds between indefinite numbers of atoms. They are indiscriminate in their operation and find their only limitation in the fact that the sizes of atoms limit the number that can cluster about any one atom. Since those forces all fall off with increasing distance, their bonds are strongest between nearest neighbours.

On the other hand, the discussion of covalent bonds in the last three chapters has emphasized the bonding of atoms in pairs. The covalent bonding of more than two atoms into a polyatomic molecule has been pictured as occurring by the formation of links between adjacent atoms, each welded by the localized behaviour of electrons that remain associated with no more than two atoms.

For most molecules this is a useful habit of thought. As the last chapter has shown, it provides a way of thinking that can give a good account of many of the facts of chemistry. The structural diagrams drawn by chemists formalize this way of thinking, and organic chemistry has profited from it especially. By such diagrams chemists can symbolize the results of their analyses of many very complicated organic compounds, and can use them to direct synthetic procedures for preparing the compounds in the laboratory, linking one atom or group of atoms to another in a predictable way, step by step.

But sometimes the picture of localized bonding fails. Sometimes the chemical composition of a molecule and the spatial arrangement of its atoms do not dictate an unambiguous choice between two or more possible bonding schemes. In such a case there are two ways of modifying the picture of localized bonding.

One way is to examine molecular orbitals for the electrons that take all the atoms into account at once and not just in pairs. Then the bonding electrons can be pictured in states that are delocalized from any particular pair of atoms in the molecule. Such delocalization merely carries further the delocalization already visualized in forming the bond between two atoms. There the electrons are already removed from strict allegiance to the atoms and are shared between them.

This observation points to an analogy that suggests the second way of modifying the picture of localized bonding. As the last two chapters have shown, a good picture of the bond between two atoms can be made by examining the properties of the individual atoms. In a somewhat analogous way, a good picture can be made of the behaviour of the ambiguously constructed molecules by thinking of their structures as combinations of alternative schemes of bonding, all taken at once—as *mesomers* of several simply linked structures. This device has the great advantage of preserving as well as possible the structural schemes that have proved to be so useful throughout chemistry.

The classic example of a molecule with an ambiguous structure is benzene, C_6H_6. All six carbon atoms, and all six hydrogen atoms, behave alike in chemical reactions, and any proposed bonding scheme must be consistent with that fact. In 1865 Friedrich Kekulé guessed that the carbon atoms are bonded together in a regular hexagonal ring, and that one hydrogen atom is bonded to each of them (Fig. 8.1(a)). The guess has since been confirmed:

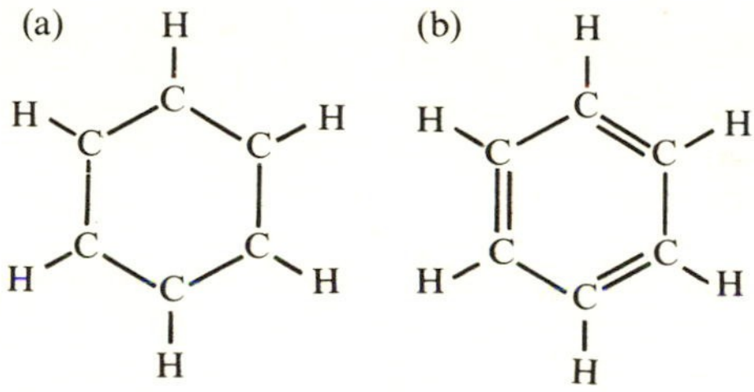

FIG. 8.1. In the molecule of benzene (a) all hydrogen atoms and all carbon atoms are coplanar. A bonding structure that satisfies the valency requirements is (b).

the ring is planar, and the hydrogen atoms are coplanar with the ring.

Since hydrogen has the valency one and carbon the valency four, a satisfactory bonding scheme might be that shown in Fig. 8.1(b). But the scheme is inconsistent with many chemical observations on benzene—with its chemical derivatives, for example, in which some of the hydrogen atoms are replaced by other atoms or groups of atoms. Three dichlorobenzenes can be prepared, which are distinguishable in melting point, boiling point, and the like. Their structures can be identified with those of Fig. 8.2(a). But two different orthodichlorobenzenes have never been observed; and Fig. 8.2(b) shows that there should be two distinguishable compounds if the double bond were distinguishable from the single bond. In other sorts of compounds, double bonds are readily distinguishable from single bonds—they differ in length, for example (Fig. 7.13). Much evidence has conspired to force the conclusion that the bonds between the carbon atoms are all alike.

The only way to make these bonds look alike, and yet satisfy the valency of four for carbon, is to draw the structure shown in Fig. 8.3(a), in which each carbon atom is singly bonded to a carbon atom across the ring. Interpreted literally, such a scheme is odd, for the distance across the ring is 2·8 Å and the usual single-bond distance between two carbon atoms is

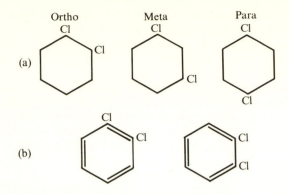

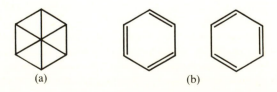

Fig. 8.2. Three distinguishable molecules (a) are ortho-, meta-, and para-dichlorobenzene. Two distinguishable orthodichlorobenzenes (b) with the bonding sequences Cl—C—C—Cl and Cl—C=C—Cl have never been observed. Carbon atoms are at all corners of the hexagons.

only 1·54 Å. The scheme is equally odd if it is interpreted as symbolizing a concentration of six bonding electrons near the middle of the ring, for the mutual repulsions in such an electronic concentration would assist the attractions of the carbon nuclei to spread the concentration out from the middle. The molecule is therefore regarded as a mesomer of a group of structures, of which the principal members are the two structures shown in Fig. 8.3(b).

Sometimes chemists refer to such a combination as a *resonance combination*. It is a poorly chosen term, but it has become deeply lodged in their speech about compounds like benzene. They mean that the wave functions for the electrons can be approximated by a sum of the wave functions for those structures, in the way that Chapter 6 pictured the wave function for the hydrogen molecule as a sum of atomic wave functions.

Alternatively, the bonding can be pictured in terms of wave functions for an electron traversing all six carbon atoms, in the way that Chapter 5 displayed wave functions for an electron in the presence of two attractive centres. For

Fig. 8.3. The 'Bamberger structure' (a) for benzene is less reasonable than a combination of two participating 'Kekulé structures' (b).

this purpose the benzene molecule would be visualized as in Fig. 8.4. Localized single bonds, between hydrogen atoms and carbon atoms, and between adjacent pairs of carbon atoms, employ three of the four bonding electrons of each carbon atom, and leave a total of six electrons to occupy the spatially extended orbitals.

Again a one-dimensional model, using delta wells to represent the atoms, provides a simple illustration of how the inquiry might proceed. The appendix to this chapter finds six independent wave functions, three bonding and three antibonding, for the problem. The six electrons can occupy, by spin-opposed pairs, the three bonding orbitals. It turns out that the resulting collection

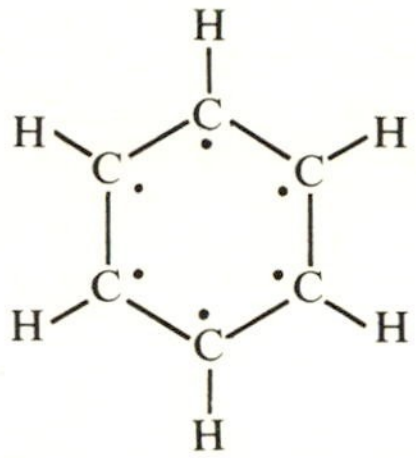

FIG. 8.4. The extended wave functions of the molecule of benzene must accommodate one electron from each carbon atom, left over after the other three electrons of principal quantum number 2 have been used to form localized bonds.

of electronic states can have a lower energy than a collection of spatially localized bonds would have.

It is not surprising that the participation of different bonding structures is a common occurrence in molecules. When more than two nuclei are available to the electrons, it would be more surprising if the electrons did not use the additional space in which their potential energy is low to reduce their kinetic energy. The extent to which this happens, however, is restricted by the electronic behaviour summarized in the exclusion principle. That behaviour does not prevent all the electrons from occupying wave functions that are identical but in different positions in space. Insofar as the wave functions overlap, however, they will seldom be identical; some will have higher energy and some will have lower energy than localized wave functions would have. Thus it is not easy to predict what molecules will delocalize their electrons to a significant extent.

The experimental evidence for delocalized bonding comes from many properties of molecules of which perhaps the most important are (1) the geometrical arrangements of their component atoms, (2) their total energies, and (3) their dipole moments. The regular hexagonal configuration of benzene illustrates the first of these sorts of evidence. The second sort of evidence comes from thermochemical measurements—measurements of the heats absorbed and evolved in chemical reactions with other sorts of molecules.

By suitable addition of those heats, the energies of the molecules can often be calculated. When delocalization is unimportant, it turns out that the energy of a molecule can be calculated as a sum of energies ascribed to its component localized bonds. Conversely, when the energy is lower than that, the difference can usually be ascribed to delocalization.

In the case of benzene the thermochemical value of the energy required to disperse the molecule into its component atoms is 1041·12 kcal per mole.† The energies required to break localized bonds, determined from experimental work on many molecules in which delocalization is negligible, are $E_{C-H} = 85·56$, $E_{C-C} = 62·77$, and $E_{C=C} = 101·16$ kcal per mole. If the

(a)   (b)

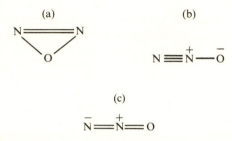

(c)

FIG. 8.5. For nitrous oxide, the structure (a) is impossible because the molecule is linear, and the structures (b) and (c) may both participate because the dipole moment of the molecule is almost zero.

benzene molecule had one of the Kekulé structures (Fig. 8.3(b)), the calculated energy would be $3E_{C-C} + 3E_{C=C} + 6E_{C-H} = 1005·15$ kcal per mole. The difference of 35·97 kcal per mole is called the 'experimental value of the resonance energy' of benzene.

Notice that the idea of *resonance energy* is somewhat loose. It is the amount by which the true energy of the molecule is less than the energy that you think it would have if its electronic structure corresponded with some arrangement of localized bonds. The arrangement of localized bonds that you pick for comparison is a best guess based on a knowledge of chemistry, and usually chemistry severely restricts the range of reasonable guessing. The resonance energy remains as the difference between the true energy and that of your best guess.

To see how the dipole moment can give evidence of the importance of delocalization in a molecule, turn to a molecule very different from benzene: nitrous oxide, N_2O, the 'laughing gas' of anesthetic practice. Paying attention only to the valency three of nitrogen and the valency two of oxygen, one can propose for this molecule the arrangement of bonds shown in Fig. 8.5(a). But the atoms in the molecule are not triangularly arranged in fact; they are arranged in a straight line in the order NNO. This fact poses a problem in

† See Discussion 3.1, Units.

bonding that offers a splendid opportunity to play a game, dear to many chemical theorists, in which electrons are pushed about on paper to portray reasonable bonding arrangements.

One possible arrangement is suggested by the fact that the molecule looks like a molecule of nitrogen that has attached an atom of oxygen at one end. In the nitrogen molecule (Fig. 7.9) three of the five electrons of principal quantum number 2 in each nitrogen atom are exchanging places, to form a triple bond, leaving two electrons in each atom unexploited in bonding. And an oxygen atom has an unexploited 2p orbital that could accommodate two electrons.

Suppose then that the so-called *nonbonding pair* of electrons from a nitrogen atom spend half their time on the oxygen atom, and thus form a bond. To assist its analysis, the formation of this bond could be regarded as taking place in two stages. In stage No. 1 a nitrogen atom in the molecule loses one electron to the oxygen atom, and in stage No. 2 the remaining unpaired electron on the nitrogen atom exchanges with the new unpaired electron on the oxygen atom to form a single covalent bond. Stage No. 1 makes the nitrogen molecule into a nitrogen-molecule ion of charge $+e$ and the oxygen atom into an oxygen ion of charge $-e$. Stage No. 2 leaves these net charges unchanged, and thus the molecule would have a large dipole moment. Nitrogen atoms very frequently form such *donor-acceptor* or *dative* bonds. The proposed structure is shown in Fig. 8.5(b).

Now in fact, nitrous oxide has a vanishingly small dipole moment. Hence the proposed structure becomes credible only by supposing that it is accompanied by a participating structure that cancels the dipole moment. It is easy to believe that an equally important arrangement might be that shown in Fig. 8.5(c). There an electron is visualized as moving from the central nitrogen atom to the other nitrogen atom rather than the oxygen atom. This structure can be regarded as using one of the polar forms of the nitrogen molecule to provide a bond in which the oxygen atom has its usual valency of two. In fact nitrous oxide is often described today as a *resonance hybrid* of the structures shown in Fig. 8.5(b) and (c), with no net dipole moment.†

There are many organic molecules that resemble benzene in the type of bonding that links their carbon atoms. In the molecules (Fig. 8.6) of naphthalene, anthracene, phenanthrene, and perylene, for example, the electrons not engaged in localized single bonds are able to range over the entire molecule. If benzene rings are fused together in such a fashion as this indefinitely, the structure in Fig. 8.7 arises; it is one plane of atoms in a crystal of graphite. The electrons can now range throughout the plane, and

---

† Here the term 'resonance' is especially inappropriate. The term refers to an analogy between, on the one hand two similar oscillators that are weakly coupled, and on the other hand two similar electronic states whose wave functions overlap. Here, however, the two states are not similar.

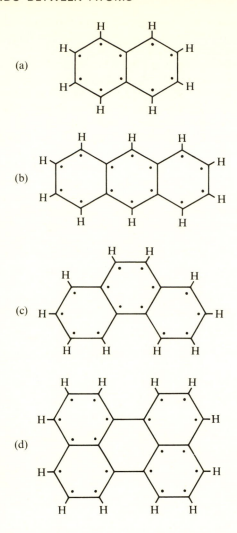

FIG. 8.6. The molecules of (a) naphthalene, (b) anthracene, (c) phenanthrene, and (d) perylene. Carbon atoms are at all corners and intersections in the diagrams.

indeed a single crystal of graphite shows a relatively high electrical conductivity in directions parallel to the planes, and a relatively low conductivity perpendicular to the planes. These electrons, and those others that form the localized single bonds, are binding the carbon atoms together tightly in the planes; the carbon–carbon distance (1·42 Å) is like that in benzene. Between

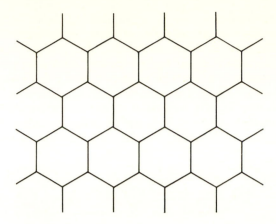

FIG. 8.7. Graphite contains sheets of 'fused' benzene rings.

the planes the binding is largely by dispersion forces, and the shortest carbon–carbon distance is 3·4 Å.

Thus one can think of graphite as a material that has gone part of the way toward a metal. And there is another way of looking at the behaviour of the relatively free electrons in graphite that helps in visualizing the bonding in metals. Consider the free electrons in graphite, one electron per atom, as trying to form localized electron-pair bonds between neighbouring pairs of atoms. Count the bonds per atom that the electrons try to form, and compare that number with the number of electrons per atom that are available to to form the bonds.

As Fig. 8.7 shows, each carbon atom has three nearest neighbours. Since each of the attempted bonds would connect two atoms, the number of such bonds per atom would be 3/2. If the bonds were localized electron-pair bonds, each would accommodate two electrons, and thus saturated bonding would use $2 \times 3/2 = 3$ electrons per atom. But there is only one of the free electrons available per atom. Hence these bonds are *electron-deficient*: the demand for electrons exceeds the supply.

Now make a similar count for an alkali metal, such as sodium. The alkali metals crystallize in a structure that gives to each atom eight nearest neighbours, and thus the number of bonds per atom is four. Since an alkali metal atom has only one electron in its outermost shell, the number of electrons available per atom is one, whereas eight would be needed to supply each bond with a pair of electrons. The large electron deficiency gives the electrons much freedom.

But the ideas of resonance and of electron-deficient bonding are not equivalent ideas: nitrous oxide is a good example of resonance without deficiency. The outermost electronic shell of each nitrogen atom—the shell with principal quantum number 2—contains five electrons, and that of the oxygen atom contains six. In order to check the molecule for electron deficiency, these electrons can be paired off in the way shown in Fig. 8.8(a), to suggest that some electrons stay on the atoms and some participate in localized electron-pair bonds. This scheme of pairing leaves two electrons, one on each extreme atom, to participate in a nonlocalized bond.

But if this were the true bonding structure, the system could make no distinction between one N—O bond and the other. It would pull the nuclei into a configuration symmetrical with respect to those two bonds, and there

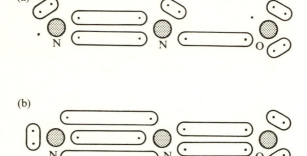

Fig. 8.8. In the electron-pairing scheme (a) for nitrous oxide, the two electrons left over would form a bond that would pull the molecule into the configuration of Fig. 8.5(a). Scheme (b) would invoke a high-energy state on the central nitrogen atom.

would be no electron deficiency in either. In short, the molecule would take the form of Fig. 8.5(a).

Since the three atoms have in fact the linear arrangement NNO, the two electrons of the *nonbonding pair* on the central atom must participate in the bonding. This provides four electrons and two nearest-neighbour bonds for them to form, and again the counting scheme leaves no electron deficiency. But the electrons still cannot be paired in localized bonds, by such a scheme as that in Fig. 8.8(b), because the scheme would require five electron pairs to find suitable orbitals on the central nitrogen atom. Four pairs of electrons use up the states with principal quantum number 2, and the fifth pair would be forced into a state of much higher energy, with principal quantum number 3.

Thus in the case of nitrous oxide either the idea of several participating states, or the idea of delocalized bonding such as Discussion 8.1 describes, is essential to explain the properties of the molecule. As the properties of other molecules are measured in increasing diversity and with greater refinement, it is steadily becoming more evident that the idea of strictly

Discussion 8.1

DELOCALIZED BONDS IN NITROUS OXIDE

In order to examine the states of delocalized electrons that participate in the bonding of nitrous oxide, seek wave functions that are appropriate to three attractive centres in a line.

Visualize removing four electrons, one from each of the extreme atoms and two from the central atom; then find wave functions in the field of the resulting ions; and finally put back the electrons one by one.

Thinking of the problem in one dimension, and approximating the ions by delta wells, you would look at the picture in Fig. 8.9. The two end wells are identical, an approximation suggested by the fact that the molecule has no dipole moment, and the central well is twice as deep as the end wells, because two electrons have been removed from the central atom.

You expect to find three wave functions, much as you found two for the case of two wells in Chapter 5. One of the functions will have no nodes, one will have one node, and one will

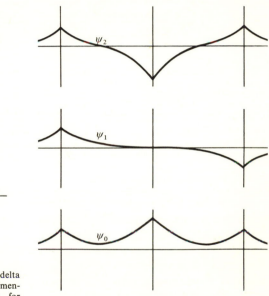

FIG. 8.9. A scheme of delta wells to form a one-dimensional approximation for the wave functions of four bonding electrons in nitrous oxide.

FIG. 8.10. Expected form of wave functions for the wells of Fig. 8.9, with energies $E_0 < E_1 < E_2$.

have two nodes; and you expect that the corresponding energies will increase, becoming less negative, in that order. Since the problem is symmetrical about the central well, you can sketch the expected forms of the wave functions as in Fig. 8.10.

Now put back the four electrons. Two can go into the lowest-energy wave function and two into the function of next higher energy, leaving the highest-energy function unoccupied. In the second of these functions you can see quite clearly a reflection of the picture that the idea of resonance also produced—the picture of polar states with extra electrons on the two extreme atoms. Squaring that function makes clear that it represents a state in which the electron density is greatest at the extreme wells and vanishes at the central well. Of course the total electron-density distribution of the four electrons will be proportional to the sum of the squares of this function and the function of lowest energy.

localized covalent bonding is only a first approximation to the facts. When it is removed from one atom, to participate in bonding with another, an electron has some probability, if only a small one, of finding itself anywhere within the molecule of which those atoms form a part.

PROBLEMS

8.1   Write the Kekulé structures of the molecules (Fig. 8.6) of naphthalene (three structures), anthracene (four structures), and phenanthrene (five structures).

8.2   Why can you not in principle determine the resonance energy of nitrous oxide relative to the structure of Fig. 8.5(b) by comparing a measured energy of nitrous oxide with the sum of the energy of the nitrogen molecule $E_{N \equiv N}$ and the energy E_{N-O} of the usual single bond between nitrogen and oxygen as found for example in such molecules as hydroxylamine, H_2NOH?

8.3   Use the electron-deficient bonding picture to explain qualitatively why the closest carbon–carbon distance in benzene is shorter than in graphite.

APPENDIX

A DELTA-WELL MODEL FOR BENZENE

A one-dimensional delta-well model for benzene can be constructed and studied in much the same way that the similar model for the hydrogen-molecule ion was studied in Chapter 5. Imagine six delta wells evenly spaced along one coordinate. In this case the system is cyclic, but if you imagine it to be cut at one point and spread out along a line, you can preserve its cyclic character in the calculation by matching the wave function at the end of the line to that at the beginning of the line.

It is helpful to use 'local coordinates' in the problem, describing the wave function between each pair of wells by a coordinate whose origin is midway between the wells (Fig. 8.11). As in Chapter 5, the wave function for the coordinate x_j everywhere between its bounding wells will be

$$\psi_j = A_j e^{-kx_j} + B_j e^{kx_j}, \tag{A8.1}$$

where A_j and B_j are constants and $k^2 \equiv -E$ is the energy. Matching ψ_j and ψ_{j+1} at the point where $x_j = R/2$ and $x_{j+1} = -R/2$, you obtain

$$A_j e^{-kR/2} + B_j e^{kR/2} = A_{j+1} e^{kR/2} + B_{j+1} e^{-kR/2}. \tag{A8.2}$$

The discontinuity in derivatives across the delta well at the same point can be evaluated by the relations

$$\frac{d\psi_{j+1}}{dx_{j+1}}\bigg|_{x_{j+1} = -R/2} - \frac{d\psi_j}{dx_j}\bigg|_{x_j = +R/2} = -\eta\psi_j(R/2) \tag{A8.3}$$

where η is the parameter specifying the well:

$$-kA_{j+1}e^{kR/2} + kB_{j+1}e^{-kR/2} + kA_j e^{-kR/2} - kB_j e^{kR/2}$$
$$= -\eta(A_j e^{-kR/2} + B_j e^{kR/2}). \tag{A8.4}$$

Eqns (A8.2) and (A8.4) are a pair that determine A_{j+1} and B_{j+1} in terms of A_j and B_j; they can be rearranged to read

$$A_{j+1} = (\alpha+1)e^{-kR}A_j + \alpha B_j,$$
$$B_{j+1} = -\alpha A_j - (\alpha-1)e^{kR}B_j, \tag{A8.5}$$

where α denotes $\eta/2k$.

Rewrite (A8.5), substituting $j-1$ for j throughout, and then eliminate B_{j+1}, B_j and B_{j-1} from the four equations, to obtain a relation involving only the A's:

$$A_{j+1} + [(\alpha-1)e^{kR} - (\alpha+1)e^{-kR}]A_j + A_{j-1} = 0. \tag{A8.6}$$

This is a linear finite-difference equation in the independent variable j. Its solutions can be found by comparing it with the trigonometric identity,

$$\cos(j+1)\theta + \cos(j-1)\theta = 2\cos j\theta \cos\theta. \tag{A8.7}$$

Clearly its solutions can be taken as

$$A_j = A\cos j\theta, \tag{A8.8}$$

where

$$\cos\theta = \tfrac{1}{2}[(\alpha+1)e^{-kR} - (\alpha-1)e^{kR}] \equiv \cosh kR - \alpha\sinh kR. \tag{A8.9}$$

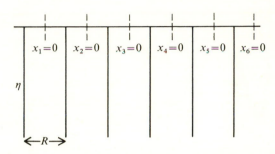

FIG. 8.11. A scheme of six similar delta wells, and local coordinates, to calculate the nonlocalized wave functions for a one-dimensional model of benzene.

The cyclic condition must now be applied to this solution. That condition requires that the A's and B's repeat themselves at the seventh set ($A_7 = A_1, B_7 = B_1$) and this is accomplished in the solution (A8.8) by requiring

$$\theta = \frac{n\pi}{7}, \tag{A8.10}$$

where n is any integer. All the distinct solutions are provided by $n = 1, 2, 3, 4, 5, 6$; the solutions for larger values of n only duplicate these. Thus there are six independent wave functions for the system of six wells, just as there are two—the symmetric and antisymmetric functions—for the two wells used in discussing the hydrogen-molecule ion.

The energy corresponding to each of these wave functions can be obtained from (A8.9). For each value of n in (A8.10) for θ, (A8.9) gives k, and thus the energy $E = -k^2$, as a function of the interatomic separation R and the nature of the atom, η. Fig. 8.12 plots the roots of this equation, and shows as dotted lines the roots of the corresponding equation (Chapter 5, eqn (A5.9) for the wave functions for two wells.

Notice that, alike in the two-well and the six-well cases, half the wave functions have energies that decrease and half have energies that increase with decreasing separation of the wells: half are *bonding* functions and half are *antibonding* functions. The fact that all the energies in the six-well case become infinite for very small R reflects an artificiality of the model. Since the model is cyclical and one dimensional, it shrinks the space available to the electrons as R decreases. There is no way for an

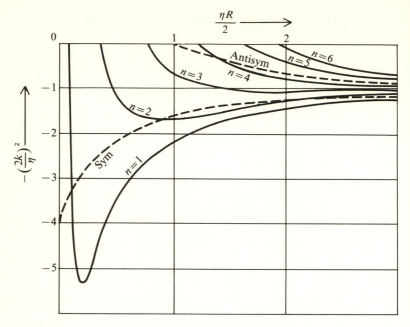

FIG. 8.12. Energy (vertically) versus bond length (horizontally) in the six wave functions of the one-dimensional cyclic delta-well model for benzene. Dotted lines are the energies of the wave functions for two delta wells (Fig. 5.8).

electron to increase its de Broglie wavelength and thus decrease its kinetic energy by spending more time away from the space between the wells, as there is in the open-ended model of two wells. The real three-dimensional case would not afford such minima in the electronic energy as this model exhibits.

The actual interatomic spacing R in molecules like benzene, however, is sufficiently large to make this defect of the model negligible. Thus it is significant to compare the energy of six electrons in the cyclical model with the energy they would have if they were in localized bonds of the same length. You can think, for example, of comparing the energies of the two structures of Fig. 8.13 for benzene.

Since the scale in Fig. 8.12 is in atomic units, using the reduced variables $\eta R/2$ and $-(2k/\eta)^2$, it gives energies and distances directly in atomic units for hydrogen, whose 1s state can be represented by a well with $\eta = 2$. You can determine a suitable value for a well to represent a 2p state of carbon by taking $\eta = 2\sqrt{(I_C/I_H)}$, where

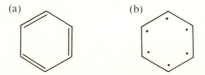

FIG. 8.13. The *resonance energy* of benzene is the difference between the energies of the molecule when six of its electrons are engaged (a) in localized and (b) in non-localized bonding.

I_C/I_H is the ratio of the first ionization potentials of carbon and hydrogen: $I_H = 13\cdot59$ eV, $I_C = 11\cdot27$ eV, $I_C/I_H = 0\cdot828$. Neglecting the electrostatic interactions of the electrons with one another but bearing in mind the exclusion principle, you can calculate for various values of R the energy of two electrons (of opposite spin) in each of the three lowest-energy six-well wave functions, add them, and compare the result with six times the energy in the symmetric two-well function of Chapter 5, plotted again in Fig. 8.12. Over a large range of R the difference turns out for carbon to be about $0\cdot1$ atomic unit $= 1\cdot35$ eV $= 31$ kcal per mole in favour of the cyclical bonding.

This difference corresponds well with the difference of $34\cdot4$ kcal per mole that has been found by inference from the heats of combustion of organic compounds, and that is called by chemists the 'resonance energy' of benzene. But the correspondence should not be taken very seriously, in light of the obvious shortcomings of the model for which it is derived.

PROBLEMS

8.4   Show that the wave functions for the cyclical set of six delta wells have $n-1$ zeros.

8.5   Anyone who has studied abstract algebra may recognize a way to think about (A8.5) that has attractive mathematical elegance. Think of A_j and B_j as the Cartesian components of a vector $\mathbf{R}_j$ in a two-dimensional 'space'. Then think of (A8.5) as embodying an 'operation' T that transforms the vector $\mathbf{R}_j$ into the vector $\mathbf{R}_{j+1}$. Finally think of the cyclic property of the system under study as requiring that six successive performances of the operation carry the vector to identity with the initial vector; in other words, $T^6 = I$, where I is the identity operation. Use these ideas to derive the results obtained by the use of finite-difference equations in the appendix.

9. The World's Materials

OUR study of bonding could continue indefinitely, refining our calculations, specializing them to interesting cases, and examining the results of applying increasingly sophisticated tools for studying molecules experimentally. Instead of pursuing that route, stand back to consider the insights gained by this brief inquiry into the nature and variety of the bonds between atoms.

Surely the most important insight is the realization that a quarter millenium of experiment and reflection has accomplished the charge that Sir Isaac Newton laid upon 'experimental Philosophy'. By ascribing to interatomic bonds an electrostatic explanation, a good account can be given of the bonds so far encountered, in all their variety. To encompass by a single explanation so great a span as that separating the vapour of salt and a crystal of diamond is a remarkable vindication of Occam's razor, 'Let not hypotheses be multiplied beyond the necessity to explain the facts.'

Despite the common origin of these bonds, however, their variety is sufficient to suggest the convenience of classifying bonds in the way developed in Chapter 2. Subsequent chapters have amplified the meanings of those classifications, and quantified their terms, sufficiently to make profitable another survey of how the materials of the world fit into them.

It is interesting, for example, to compare the bonding of atoms in the worlds of the living and the inanimate. Living matter is made of *organic compounds*, and their great diversity is accountable to the unique ability of carbon atoms to bond covalently to one another. Each molecule of an organic compound is built upon a skeleton of carbon atoms tightly bonded in rings and branching chains. Most of the links in these chains are localized electron-pair bonds, hybridized in the ways described at the end of Chapter 7. The hydrogen atoms, and occasionally also atoms of oxygen and nitrogen, are tied to the skeleton, again by covalent bonds. The chainlike structure of the hydrocarbon *n*-octane (Fig. 9.1) exemplifies the simplest sort of organic compound.

Since oxygen and nitrogen atoms are more electronegative than carbon, their bonds to carbon atoms have an ionic ingredient. That ingredient gives the molecules local dipole moments, whose interaction with the similar dipole moments in neighbouring molecules makes the molecules cohere.

The links in such a chain as that shown in Fig. 9.1 are made of sp^3 hybrid bonds; and since such a bond is cylindrically symmetrical about its axis, groups of atoms can rotate about any of those bonds. Hence, even though the bond holds its two atoms quite tightly at a fixed distance, and stands quite rigidly at the tetrahedral angle to the other three bonds formed by the same atom, the molecule as a whole has considerable flexibility (Fig. 9.2).

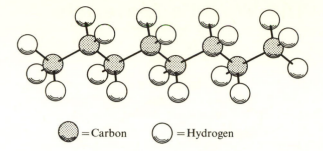

= Carbon   ◯ = Hydrogen

FIG. 9.1. The chain of carbon atoms in the hydrocarbon, *n*-octane (C_8H_{18}), linked by sp³ bonds, exemplifies the simplest type of organic compounds. This and the succeeding diagrams of molecules are not drawn to scale. They are intended only to show the bonding connexions between the atoms, and some of the spatial relations that those connexions imply.

Certainly in a vapour of such a material, and probably even in its liquid form or in solution, the molecules are constantly flexing and coiling with internal thermal motions. In the solid form of such a substance, the molecules will adopt the positions and shapes that enable them to pack together most closely under the influence of the weak van der Waals forces that bond them to one another. But since the molecules remain flexible, solid organic materials are often soft and pliant.

In some organic compounds, however, the linking within each molecule is so patterned that no flexibility is left: the requirements that the bonds have constant lengths and stand at tetrahedral angles constrain all the atoms to fixed relative positions about which they can only quiver. Diamond (Fig. 2.3), in which carbon atoms are bonded by sp³ bonds, is a conspicuous example of the resulting rigidity. For the same reason the molecules of the hydrocarbon adamantane (Fig. 9.3) behave much like inflexible spheres.

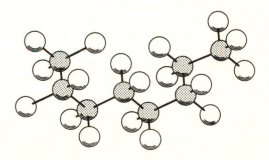

FIG. 9.2. Even though the bond angles and bond lengths are fixed in *n*-octane, groups of atoms can rotate freely about any C—C bond, as long as they do not get in one another's way.

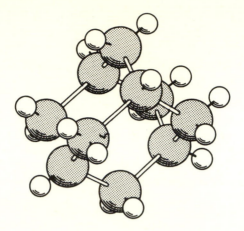

FIG. 9.3. In the hydrocarbon adamantane ($C_{10}H_{16}$) the pattern of sp³ bonding restrains the atoms quite rigidly.

In making the modern plastics this principle is used to provide the desired degree of stiffness. Many plastics are based upon molecules whose skeleton is an extremely long chain of carbon atoms. Polythene, for example, consists of hydrocarbon molecules like those of *n*-octane in which the chain (Fig. 9.4) contains several hundred carbon atoms instead of eight. Rubber, though a more complicated structure, is essentially similar. The art of vulcanizing rubber is in large part the art of cross-linking these chains (Fig. 9.5) in order to decrease their flexibility. The links, made by introducing sulphur atoms, can be multiplied to the number producing 'hard rubber', in which the flexibility of the original rubber has nearly vanished. The vulcanizing art appeared long before an explanatory theory of cross-linking, but now that theory can be used to provide directives for the design of molecules that can be deliberately cross-linked to any desired extent.

In another important class of plastics, including nylon, the skeletal chain is made partly of nitrogen atoms, and one of the carbon atoms adjacent to each nitrogen atom bears an oxygen atom closely bonded to it, as Fig. 9.6 shows. Because of the differences in the electronegativities of carbon, nitrogen, and oxygen, the covalent bonds in this part of the molecule have large ionic

FIG. 9.4. A molecule of the modern plastic polythene $(CH_2)_n$ consists of a chain like that shown in Fig. 9.1, continued through several hundred atoms.

Fig. 9.5. Cross-linking long molecular chains by covalent bonds increases rigidity of a plastic.

ingredients, which produce a local dipole moment. The isolated dipole moments along the chain interact with the dipole moments in adjacent chains to provide cross-linkings that, though weaker than those of covalent bonds, are stronger than the dispersion forces that hold together the molecules of a hydrocarbon. The total strength of the force holding molecule to molecule can be controlled by spacing the dipolar atomic groups suitably along the chain.

There is another way of controlling the strength of the intermolecular forces in these nitrogen-bearing plastics—a way that gives insight into some of the properties of the proteins that compose the flesh and muscle of animals. The forces can be weakened by attaching short side chains to the principal chain of the molecular skeleton and so holding the dipoles in adjacent skeletons further apart.

In the skeletal chain of the proteins, each pair of units that contribute a local dipole moment—the NH and CO units—is separated from the next pair by only one carbon atom. But each of these carbon atoms carries a relatively large side group (Fig. 9.7). The side groups vary in nature from one protein to another, and they also vary from point to point along the principal chain of any one molecule. Some of these side groups are simple chains, others are rings. Thus the strong attractions between the numerous dipoles are weakened in ways that have much subtle variety, and the varying shapes of the side groups impose additional variety on the ways in which any of the molecules can coil within itself and can pack together with its fellow molecules.

Turning from the organic world, dominated by compounds of carbon, we find the inorganic world dominated by compounds of silicon. At first one might expect to find silicon playing precisely the part of carbon. It falls directly beneath carbon in the same column of the periodic table, and it has four bonding electrons that could form hybrid bonds. In fact, however, two silicon atoms never bond to each other directly in a mineral. Each silicon

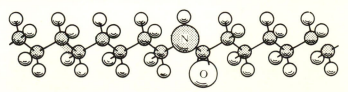

Fig. 9.6. In plastics of the polyamide type, the skeletal chain acquires local dipole moments at the points where the (NH)–(CO) configuration occurs.

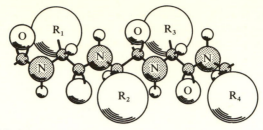

Fig. 9.7. A protein is a polyamide with closely spaced (NH)—(CO) configurations and with side groups that vary in nature and size. Typical groups are H—, $(CH_3)_2CH.CH_2$—, and $HO.C_6H_4$—CH_2—.

atom is bonded directly to four oxygen atoms by sp^3 bonds. One can picture each silicon atom at the centre of a tetrahedron whose corners are occupied by oxygen atoms.

In isolation such a tetrahedron has a strong electron affinity. Since the bond to the silicon atom employs only one of the bonding electrons of an oxygen atom, there is room in each for one more electron in an atomic orbital of principal quantum number 2. Hence an isolated SiO_4 group readily forms the negative orthosilicate ion, SiO_4^{4-} (Fig. 9.8).

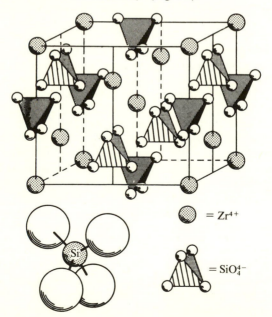

$\bigcirc$ = Zr^{4+}

$\triangle$ = SiO_4^{4-}

Fig. 9.8. The SiO_4 group takes a central position, as a structural base in the inorganic world, that is somewhat analogous to the position of the carbon atom in the organic world. In some minerals (for example, zircon) it stands as a tetravalent ion, here shown as a tetrahedron with corner oxygens.

More often, however, one finds silicon atoms bonding to one another through oxygen bridges: a bridging oxygen atom forms covalent bonds with two silicon atoms. In the resulting structures one can find interesting analogies to organic compounds. For example, a chain of the form —Si—O—Si—O bears some resemblance to a chain of the form —C—C—.

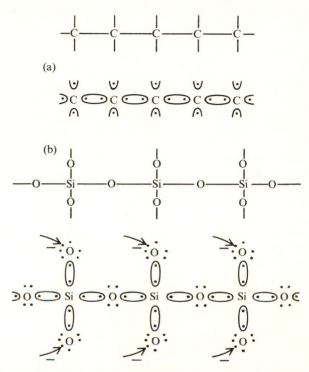

Fig. 9.9. In most organic compounds, the carbon skeletons (a) are clothed by covalently bonded atoms, so that the molecules are held to one another by van der Waals forces. In most minerals, the silica skeletons (b) bear a net negative charge, and the minerals are held together by the ionic forces between skeletons and positive ions.

But, as Fig. 9.9 points out, the carbon skeleton, by clothing itself with covalently bonded atoms, becomes electrostatically neutral. In the silicate skeleton, on the other hand, the oxygen atoms that are not engaged in bridging acquire electrons, so that the entire skeleton becomes a negative ion. In a mineral these electrons are contributed by metal atoms, which thus become positive ions. In the mineral diopside equal numbers of calcium and magnesium atoms furnish the metal ions. The entire mineral is held together, therefore, by ionic bonds whose strength greatly exceeds that of the van der Waals forces holding the organic solids together. The positively charged metal ions distribute themselves among the negatively charged silicate skeletons however their sizes and the ionic forces make most favourable.

Often the Si—O—Si—O— links form rings or sheets instead of chains. In the mineral benitoite, rings are closed by three SiO groups, and each ring is accompanied by a barium ion and a titanium ion. In beryl a ring of six SiO groups accommodates three beryllium ions and two aluminum ions. Just as in sodium chloride, it is impossible to identify molecular units in these minerals; one can identify only ionic units.

But, just as among the compounds of carbon, one can find among the minerals instances in which the skeleton is tightly cross-linked. Compare, for example, the crystal structure of diamond with that of cristobalite, one of the many structures adopted by silicon dioxide, whose more usual structure is quartz. As Fig. 9.10 shows, the silicon atoms occupy sites that form a diamondlike structure opened out by the bridging oxygen atoms.

From the complicated structures of the proteins and the minerals, turn finally to look at one of the simplest molecules, H_2O—a molecule that covers deeply three-quarters of the earth's surface and moistens much of the rest. Despite its apparent simplicity, it behaves in many mysterious ways. But its behaviour can be partly understood in terms of bonds discussed in the foregoing chapters.

One of the most conspicuous properties of water is that it *wets*: in other words, water molecules stick to most other molecules quite tightly. For helping to explain this property, we can make with our bonding pictures an argument running as follows. Since oxygen atoms are electronegative, their bonds to hydrogen atoms have a large ionic ingredient, as you noticed in Figs. 7.7 and 7.8. Since the two bonds are not collinear but stand at an angle of 105°, their ionic ingredients give the water molecule a large dipole moment. When a water molecule comes close to a molecule of another sort, the electric field due to its dipole moment (Fig. 4.2) induces a dipole moment in the neighbouring molecule, oriented in an attractive direction.

But in the magnitude of its wetting affinity, water shows a larger variation than this argument can explain. It shows an especially strong affinity for oxygen-bearing molecules. Indeed it wets wood and paper, whose cellulose molecules expose many oxygen atoms at their surfaces, almost irresistibly.

Here the specially strong polarizing force of protons is at work. Recall, with the aid of Fig. 9.11, that a positive ion will induce in a neighbouring neutral atom a dipole moment that is oriented in an attractive sense. The smaller the positive ion is, the nearer it can get to the electron cloud of the neutral atom, and hence the stronger will be the attraction it establishes. A proton is much the smallest of positive ions, and it can get stuck quite tightly to neutral atoms. When those are atoms of oxygen, and the proton forms part of a water molecule in which it is already attached to another oxygen atom, the proton can pull the two oxygen atoms together and bond itself almost even-handedly to both.

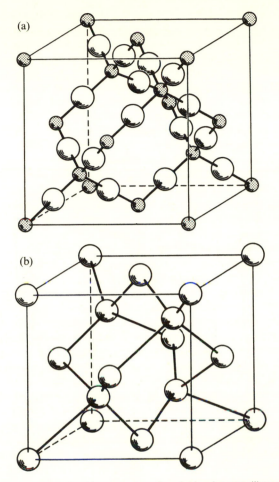

FIG. 9.10. In cristobalite (a) oxygen atoms form bridges between silicon atoms that are arranged in the same way as the carbon atoms in diamond (b).

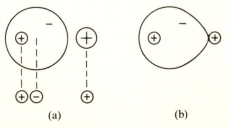

FIG. 9.11. A positive ion induces a dipole moment (a) in a neutral atom. A proton can come especially close to the electron cloud of another atom (b).

Not quite even-handedly, of course, since the oxygen atom in its parent water molecule is negatively charged and attracts it more strongly than a neutral atom. In molecules such as cellulose, however, the exposed oxygen atoms are also negatively charged. Bonds of the type exemplified by water and cellulose are often called *hydrogen bonds*. Sometimes it requires as much as 0·3 eV to break such a bond.

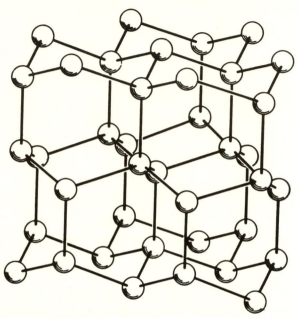

FIG. 9.12. Along the line between each neighbouring pair of oxygen atoms in ice is one hydrogen atom, which is not shown in this diagram. Most of the time it is nearer to one or the other of the oxygen atoms, and most of the time each oxygen atom has two hydrogen atoms near it.

Clearly ice is the perfect candidate for hydrogen bonding: the protons should find its oxygen atoms indistinguishable. Actually the atomic arrangement in ordinary ice—other forms of ice can be produced at high pressures—is the cage-like structure whose oxygen ions are shown in Fig. 9.12. One proton is located somewhere along each of the bonding connexions, and at any one time each oxygen ion has two protons near it. But each oxygen ion has four equivalent bonding connexions, and the protons switch their allegiance from one oxygen ion to another along those connexions. No wonder a glacier can slowly flow!

But much of the behaviour of ice still remains unexplained. Consider a snowflake, its branches replicating one another in six-fold symmetry, differently in each flake. How does it communicate, at each instant, through millions of interatomic distances, its next instant's growth plan? We do not know; the flake is one of the world's tiny beauties, and one of its large mysteries.

PROBLEMS

9.1   If there is an 'organic' world where silicon atoms (not SiO_4 groups) replace carbon atoms in proliferating 'organic compounds', would you expect to find it in a hotter or a colder environment than that provided by the Earth?

9.2   Would you attach any significance to the fact that almost all the carcenogenic (cancer-producing) hydrocarbons known at present are 'benzenoid', or in other words have bonding schemes in which the electrons are delocalized in the ways described in Chapter 8?

9.3   Protons differ from electrons primarily in having an opposite charge, and a mass about 2000 times greater; but their 'sizes' are nearly the same. Discuss the problems, arising from the bonding properties of hydrogen atoms, that would afflict the development of a 'protonics industry', comparable with the electronics industry, in which these tiny charged particles are exploited to perform comparably useful duties.

Index